Renaissance
Papers
2018

Renaissance Papers 2018

Editors
Jim Pearce and Ward J. Risvold

Associate Editor
Suzanne J. Sanders

ॐ

Published for
THE SOUTHEASTERN RENAISSANCE CONFERENCE
by
Camden House
Rochester, New York

THE SOUTHEASTERN RENAISSANCE CONFERENCE

Renaissance Papers, 2018

Copyright © 2019
The Southeastern Renaissance Conference

ISSN: 0584-4207
ISBN-13: 978-1-64014-059-2
ISBN-10: 1-64014-059-X

Published by:

Camden House
An imprint of Boydell & Brewer, Inc.
668 Mt. Hope Avenue, Rochester, NY 14620-2731, USA
www.camden-house.com

and of Boydell & Brewer Ltd.
P.O. Box 9, Woodbridge, Suffolk IP12 3DF, UK
www.boydellandbrewer.com

Printed and bound in Great Britain by
TJ International Ltd, Padstow, Cornwall

CONTENTS

Renaissance Papers

A Selection of Papers
Submitted to the
Seventy-Fifth Annual Meeting
October 19–20, 2018
UNC-Charlotte and Queens University
Charlotte, North Carolina

"One Little Room, An Everywhere": Staging Silence in London's Blackfriars and Shakespeare's *Henry VIII*

Deneen M. Senasi

I N John Donne's "The Good Morrow," love is imbued with the power to collapse time and space, conferring upon the existential limits of the one and the material bounds of the other a kind of relative elasticity—one that contracts and expands in response to the lovers' gaze because, as the speaker suggests, "love, all love of other sights controls, / And makes one little room, an everywhere."[1] While Donne's aubade takes a measure of poetic license in imagining this all-inclusive space, the argument nonetheless resonates in the cultural history of England, in particular when the power of love to enact such change aligns with other forms of authority. Indeed, the prerogatives of the sovereign are not unlike those of love, for both have the capacity to remake the perceptual landscape at the individual and collective levels, and in doing so, to insist that the subject, like a lover, accede to that presumption of control.

Donne's deeply cartographic imagination may thus be mapped onto more material "rooms," in particular those that have played an important role in the exercise of sovereign power. When a monarch dictates what can and cannot be said on a given matter, those spaces where such discourse unfolds become interwoven with that historical moment. While this might be said of many architectural artifacts, it is especially true of London's Blackfriars, where centuries of use have made "one little roome, an everywhere" in which traces of

---

[1] John Donne, "The Good Morrow," in *John Donne: The Complete English Poems*, ed. C. A. Patrides (New York: Knopf, 1991), 48.

long past speech and still resonant silences accrue. The "little room" in "The Good Morrow" evokes a limitless world transposed into an implausibly limited space through the lovers' mutual gaze. Moving beyond the familiar conceit of the microcosm (even as he employs it), Donne suggests a radical re-placement of the world in all its topographical complexity in the lovers themselves, who find in one another a place for everything and everything in *this place*, though it is important to note that the lovers I discuss in this current article, Henry VIII and Katherine of Aragon, were rather more star-crossed that those imagined in Donne's idyllic aubade.

This article takes as its premise the possibility of finding, if not everything, then at least a significant segment of pre-modern London's cultural world within "one little roome": the recurrently repurposed precinct of the Dominican Friars Preachers or Black Friars. The friary's juxtaposition of private areas for the monks' devotional practice and public space for their work as friar-preachers created an architectural orientation towards silence in dialogue with speech. That architectural, acoustic hybridity also made Blackfriars' particularly well suited to the needs of other, less spiritual constituencies. While still a functioning friary, the site served as a parliamentary and court venue under several kings and was subsequently reconfigured as a "private" playhouse: first for the Children of the Chapel Royal and other children's companies, and then for The King's Men. While it is necessarily true that two *objects* may not occupy the same space at the same time, here two (or more) *voices* may, as discrete "acoustic communities," take up residence within Blackfriars, at times coexisting, at others displacing one another within that space.

That the oft-repeated speech of kings, courtiers, and players should persist in the cultural memory preserved in such a site is hardly surprising. What is nonetheless intriguing is the degree to which such discourse is heteroglossically stratified by an array of "speaking" silences legible in both historical accounts and literary representations. Like the Chorus in *Henry V* wondering whether the Globe can "hold the vasty fields of France,"[2] in what follows I will consider what Blackfriars' acoustic field may "hold" and ask how such heteroglossic silence may be recognized and read in the

---

[2] William Shakespeare, *Henry V*, in *The Norton Shakespeare*, ed. Stephen Greenblatt, 2nd ed. (New York: Norton, 2008), 1471–1548.

historical and literary chronicling of the site. As Michel Foucault reminds us: "There is not one but many silences, and they are an integral part of the strategies that underlie and permeate discourse."[3] And while Bruce Smith has suggested "true silence does not exist," as an *idea*, it exerted tremendous power in early modern culture.[4] This paper explores that idea as it was brought to bear upon early modern subjects within Blackfriars in two related moments in the site's history: the divorce of Katherine of Aragon in 1529 (technically, an annulment proceeding) and its reenactment within the same space in Shakespeare and Fletcher's *Henry VIII*. In particular, I am interested in how the heteroglossia of silence and speech shaped the original Legatine Court proceedings and how, in the play's return to that space following the burning of the Globe in 1613, that original dialogism shaped and was itself reshaped by the play's staging of the "King's Great Matter."

While Blackfriars localizes that heteroglossia, it is present throughout the divorce's discursive space, which is marked by a kind of cultural ideation—the idea of silence as much as the phenomenon itself around which the dynamics of power coalesce and converge. The 1529 Legatine Court evocatively illustrates this field of many-voiced speech and silence, resonating with Mikhail Bakhtin's concept of "heteroglossia," a complex nexus of dialogic languages, intentions, and perspectives embedded within each concrete utterance. Bakhtin argues that the word "[forms] itself in an atmosphere of the already spoken" and is "at the same time determined by that which has not yet been said but which is needed and in fact anticipated."[5] As a series of formal speech acts, the trial was clearly "oriented toward" an "answering word," while the Legatine Court itself took place within an "atmosphere of the already spoken" in which silence constituted a crucial part of that which was "needed and in fact anticipated."

---

[3] Michel Foucault, *The History of Sexuality*, trans. Robert Hurley (New York: Vintage Books, 1990), 27.

[4] Bruce Smith, *The Acoustic World of Early Modern England* (Chicago: Univ. of Chicago Press, 1999).

[5] Mikhail Bahktin, *The Dialogic Imagination: Four Essays*, trans. Michael Holmquist and Caryl Emerson (Austin: Univ. of Texas Press, 1981), 280.

Indeed, silence came to stratify much of the speech concerning the "Great Matter." Even that euphemistic term—"the King's Great Matter"—highlights the degree to which such speech was studded with silence; marking the true nature of the enterprise as unspeakable, the phrase also emphasizes the king's authoritative possession of it. As events unfolded, an admixture of prohibitive silence and compulsory speech made the sovereigns' private lives a matter of public discourse that is reconstructed in chronicle and biography. The resonance of the unspoken suffuses this historical record, highlighting the structuring role of silence prior to the sitting of the Legatine Court. For while expressions of support from the king's subjects were certainly expected, the silencing of voices that might be raised in support of the queen was also, to use Bakhtin's words, "needed and anticipated."

To cite just one among many examples in London, silence was clearly the "answer" expected of those ordinary subjects not directly involved in the proceedings. Yet with the arrival of the papal legate, Cardinal Laurence Campeggio, in 1528, talk of the divorce was everywhere. Edward Hall's 1548 *Chronicle* notes:

> Of the coming of this Legate the common people beyng ignorant of the truth and in especial women & other that fauored the quene talked largely & sayd that the kyng would for his own pleasure haue another wife & had sent for this legate to be deuorsed fro his quene, with many folishe words, insomuche that whosoever spake against the mariage was of the comon people abhorred & reproued, which comon rumour and folishe comunicacions wer related to the king.[6]

Within the demographic of commoners' speech, in particular as Hall notes among women, an answer to the question of the divorce was becoming audible, and it was little to the king's liking. It is also worth noting that what Hall describes as these "many folishe words" from the people spill over in their condemnation to

---

[6] Edward Hall, *Hall's Chronicle; Containing the History of England, during the Reign of Henry the Fourth, and the Succeeding Monarchs, the End of the Reign of Henry the Eighth, in Which Are Particularly Described the Manners and Customs of Those Periods* (London: Printed for J. Johnson [etc.], 1809), 754.

encompass anyone in the king's service who "spake against the marriage." The suggestion that these subjects "talked largely" is diametrically opposed to the kind of silent submission the king wants and needs at this moment. Instead, such speech gives voice to precisely that which was expected to remain unspeakable in the "Great Matter," an alternative narrative in which it is the king's concupiscence not his virtue driving the divorce.

In response, Henry commanded the mayor and aldermen of London to attend him at Bridewell on November 8, 1528, where he concluded a lengthy speech by saying: "Therefore I require of you all as our trust and confidence is in you to declear our subjects our mynde and entent accordyng to our true meaning."[7] As Bakhtin suggests, here "language has been completely taken over, shot through with intentions" (293) that remain largely unspoken, perhaps unspeakable, even for a king. Interlacing the sovereign's intention with the subject's voice, Henry's speech conveys an incitement to silence for those who dare speak "largely" of the divorce. Should that incitement fail, there was also an unmistakable threat. According to the French ambassador, Du Bellay, the king declared: "If, not withstanding, he found anyone, whoever he was, who spoke in other terms than he ought to do of his Prince . . . he would let him know that he was master" and that "there was never a head so dignified but that he would make it fly."[8]

Nevertheless, the queen's arrival on June 21, 1529, elicited a cheer, since "the common people were also present at the Blackfriars court, crowding into the chamber to witness the unprecedented show."[9] In addition to its proximity to the royal residence at Bridewell, other aspects of the space made it especially amenable for trying the "Great Matter." The traditional design of Dominican friaries emphasized public interaction, providing space for the court and other spectators. The move from Holborn to Ludgate in the thirteenth century had also cemented an "intermeshing of the affairs of the friary and the Crown that was to mark the whole

---

[7] Ibid., 755.

[8] Giles Tremlett, *Catherine of Aragon: The Spanish Queen of Henry VIII* (New York: Walker Publishing Company, 2010), 268.

[9] Ibid., 268.

subsequent history of the community."[10] Among the English kings associated with the order, none made as frequent or as significant use of the friary buildings as Henry VIII.[11] Blackfriars was thus a place of power for the king, one in which royal prerogative extended into the places of the Church.

On June 21, the crier called the king and queen into the court. While Henry replied according to form, the calling of the queen met with silence. In that moment of resonant, heteroglossic entwining between the king's speech and the queen's silence, the latter necessarily echoed within Blackfriars, in its spatial framing of sovereign power. In his *Life and Death of Cardinal Wolsey*, George Cavendish details the physical preparations that structured the original staging of the "King's Great Matter" at Blackfriars: "First, there was a court placed with tables, benches, and bars, like a consistory, a place judicial for the judges to sit on. There was also a cloth of estate under which sat the king; and the queen sat some distance beneath the king: under the judges' feet sat the officers of the court."[12] Cavendish describes the crier's call and its immediate aftermath, writing:

> Then he called also the queen, by the name of Catherine Queen of England, come into the court, etc.; who made no answer to the same, but rose up incontinent out of her chair, where as she sat, and because she could not come directly to the king for the distance which severed them, she took pain to go about unto the king, kneeling down at his feet in the sight of all the court and assembly.[13]

Katherine's painstaking approach intensifies the resonance of her silence, interweaving it with the plea she is poised to make in a powerful moment of heteroglossia remembered in almost every account of the scene.

---

[10] Irwin Smith, *Shakespeare's Blackfriars Playhouse: Its History and Its Design* (New York: New York Univ. Press, 1964), 9.

[11] Ibid., 13.

[12] George Cavendish, *The Life and Death of Cardinal Wolsey Written by George Cavendish Illustrated with Portraits by Holbein* (Boston: Houghton Mifflin and Company, 1905), 81.

[13] Ibid.

Having proceeded thus far like a figure in a dumb show, she speaks, and in doing so, undercuts her husband's purported scruple concerning the marriage: "when ye had me at the first, I take God to be my judge, I was a true maid without touch of man; and whether it be true or not, I put to your conscience."[14] In contrast to his ready reply to the crier, Henry offers no response, and as one modern biographer notes, the "silence in the great hall grew painful."[15] The queen then departs. While Henry praises her virtue once in her absence, he maintains a striking silence on his wife's explosive claim.

A member of the queen's counsel, Robert Ridley, calls the court's attention to that silence, reading it in direct relationship to Katherine's speech:

> My Lords, the Cardinals; we have heard how the Queene her selfe, here in the face of the whole Court, and in the presence and hearing of the King himself, called the great God of heaven and earth to witness, that she was a pure Virgin when she first came into the Kings bed, and how she put it to his conscience, speaking unto him face to face; and if it were otherwise, we cannot imagine that either the Queen durst so appeale unto him, or the King so spoke unto (if unworthily) would not have contradicted her.[16]

Interpreting Henry's silence as filled with, rather than devoid of, meaning, Ridley identifies the heteroglossic dialogue still hanging in the air. He expresses incredulity that "meere conjectures and presumptions (should stand in competition with so great a testimony, as a Soveraigne Princes solemn attestation of her cause upon the King's conscience, and that conscience clearing her from such presumption by its own silence.)"[17] Ridley's cogent reading of Henry's silence, like the rest of what was said in the queen's defense, had little effect, underscoring again the dialogic interplay between the

---

[14] Ibid., 82.

[15] Garrett Mattingly, *Catherine of Aragon* (Boston: Little, Brown, & Company, 1941), 286–87.

[16] Thomas Bayly, *The Life & Death of That Renowned John Fisher Bishop of Rochester: Comprising the Highest and Hidden Transactions of the Church and State, in the Reign of Henry the 8th. with Divers Morall, Historicall, and Politicall Animadversions upon Cardinall Wolsey, Sir Thomas Moor, Martin Luther, with a Full Relation of Qu. Katharines Divorce* (London, 1655), 81.

[17] Ibid., 81–82.

spoken and unspoken. Though Campeggio adjourned the court without passing judgment, in time Henry would have his divorce, and Katherine would die, reduced to the title of princess dowager (which she never accepted), alone and far from court.

Shakespeare and Fletcher's play-text offers a retrospective view of these events that, as has often been noted, adheres closely to contemporary accounts. I will briefly comment on two moments where the play-text restages elements of the divorce's heteroglossic speech and silence within Blackfriars: the trial and Katherine's dream. It is worth noting, however, that the play as a whole is marked by a kind of acoustic preoccupation, as illustrated in the Prologue's fixation on hearing and being heard and subsequent scenes' anxious reflections on the consequences of artful rhetoric and unguarded speech. Indeed, the text as a whole may be read as something of an early modern sound house, one whose resonances are amplified and extended within the "one little room, an everywhere" of Blackfriars.

In his 1627 *New Atlantis*, Francis Bacon describes an experimental "sound house" akin to the heteroglossic "resounding" entailed in the trial's dramatic return to Blackfriars. Bacon writes:

> We have also sound-houses, where we practice and demonstrate all sounds, and their generation. We have harmonies which you have not, of quarter-sounds, and lesser slides of sounds. Divers instruments of music likewise to you unknown, some sweeter than any you have; together with bells and rings that are dainty and sweet. We represent small sounds as great and deep; likewise great sounds extenuate and sharp; we make divers tremblings and warblings of sounds, which in their original are entire. We represent and imitate all articulate sounds and letters; and the voices and notes of beasts and birds. We have certain helps which set to the ear do further the hearing greatly. We also have divers strange and artificial echos, reflecting the voice many times, and as it were tossing it: and some that give back the voice louder than it came."[18]

Bacon envisions an architectural instrument of amplification and alteration of a voice attenuated by space and time. This capacity to "represent and imitate all articulate sounds and letters" dovetails

---

[18] Francis Bacon, *The Great Instauration and New Atlantis*, ed. J. Weinberger (Arlington Heights, IL: AHM Publishing, 1980), 76–77.

nicely with dramaturgical practice in general and with the dynamics of the history play in particular. The sense of manipulation that Bacon's narrator revels in further suggests something of the degree to which the spoken, the unspoken, and the unspeakable appear at best as fragments within the world of the play. The rest, as Hamlet might say, "is silence," remaining just out of earshot in a cacophony of heteroglossic interplay. It is therefore remarkable to note the level of dialogic speech and silence that survives, making its way via the play's "strange echoes" once again into those spaces in which some were first articulated. Read in relation to historical accounts, the play text thus "reflects" the divorce's dialogism "many times" within the "sound house" of Blackfriars in particular, "giving back" the voice of silence even "louder than it came."

In the play's rendering of the trial, the crier calls again, and again the queen makes no answer but wends her way slowly to the king where she kneels to make her plea. Yet while the speech follows Cavendish and Holinshed closely, Katherine's assertion of virginity is not given voice. From her reminder to him that "Sir, call to mind / That I have been your wife in this obedience / Upward of twenty years, and have been blessed / By many children by you" (2.4.32–35), the action proceeds as if the words, "I was a true maid without touch of man" had never been spoken.[19] The resulting lacuna stratifies the record of Katherine's 1529 speech with a *dramaturgical* silence, which, to paraphrase Bacon, echoes strangely within the spaces of Blackfriars. While all literary reconstruction is selective, this instance appears especially compelling given the statement's heteroglot relation to Henry's silence, as read by Ridley.

Further, while Katherine's *claim* is not given *voice*, Henry's *silence* is not given *space*. Instead, that protracted break in historical accounts is filled by an exchange between Katherine and Cardinal Wolsey. Some of this material corresponds with a passage in Thomas Bayly's biography of John Fisher, one of Katherine's advocates in the trial, but does not appear at the same point in Cavendish. Even Bayly offers only a brief reference to Wolsey's animosity in Katherine's speech, but the play presents it as a full-blown dialogue. Continuing for a total of sixty-three lines in the *Norton*

---

[19] Shakespeare, *All Is True, Henry VIII*, in *The Norton Shakespeare*, ed. Stephen Greenblatt, 2nd ed. (New York: Norton, 2008), 3119–3201.

edition, the exchange is marked by its own heteroglossic interplay, complicated in this instance by a sudden suffusion of speech that overlays the silence of the historical record. As the queen and the cardinal grapple with one another, the latter appears to serve on the one hand as a proxy for the king, absorbing a wronged wife's righteous indignation, while on the other, his own speech draws attention away from Henry's prolonged silence. Unlike in historical accounts where she speaks only to the king and then departs, here Katherine gives voice to a robust indictment of the motives for the divorce, which she attributes entirely to Wolsey. In this respect, the exchange recalls Henry's command at Bridewell to "declear our subjects our mynde and entent according to our true meaning," an act of sovereign heteroglossia that Wolsey helped to orchestrate and amplify.[20] In fact, among those voices raised in support of the king's position, the cardinal's was almost certainly thoroughly mingled with that of the king, and in terms of its impact, the most resonant.

This melding of Henry's intent and Wolsey's voice leads to another intriguing moment of heteroglossia as Katherine's dramaturgical speech continues to pour into the silence of the historical accounts. Disavowing his authority in the matter of the court's proceedings, Katherine tells the Cardinal: "Therefore I say again, / I utterly abhor, yea, from my soul / Refuse you for my judge, whom yet one more / I hold my most malicious foe" (2.4.78–81). Like the "common people" Hall describes, Wolsey finds himself "abhorred and reproued" by the queen herself for lending his voice to the king's "mynde and entent." In response he tells her: "you speak not like yourself" (2.4.83), a claim that from the broader perspective found in Katherine's speech as it is recorded in contemporary accounts is not without irony. In these moments, she does indeed seem to speak in way not like her historical self, as the eloquent silence of her appearance in Blackfriars in 1529 recedes under the weight of so many words. Meanwhile, Henry maintains a silence that no one seems to notice. There is no Queen's Counsel Ridley here to call attention to it, yet it remains, adding another layer of heteroglossic stratification.

Given the oft-noted teleological end game celebrating the providential birth of Elizabeth, it is hardly surprising that such details

---

[20] Hall, *Hall's Chronicle*, 755.

are muted in the play. Yet, these "artificial echoes" are counterpoised with another alteration: the replacing of Katherine's death, from relative obscurity at Ampthill back to court, and thus, to Blackfriars. Just as the dramatic restaging of contemporary accounts amplifies heteroglossia, so too the relocation of the queen's passing stages a sight otherwise unseen within the courtly spaces of Blackfriars, one that comments on the events set in motion there in 1529. While Katherine's death takes place offstage, her dream vision, rendered as dumb show, with its compensatory narrative of a heavenly re-crowning, stages the terrible pathos of her earthly loss in complete silence. The appearance of the "six personages clad in white robes, wearing in their heads garlands of bays" (4.2.), is marked by their repeated obeisance to Katherine, emphasizing the status she died still fiercely insisting on, that of an English queen. In this way, Shakespeare and Fletcher subtly recompense Katherine for her loss, without once committing word to paper or inciting an actor to "speak largely" of her fate. By 1613, that loss was intertwined with other silences: her years of exile from court, as well as her refusal, upon pain of death, to take the 1534 Oath of Succession, naming Henry as the head of the Church and Anne Boleyn as his rightful queen.

When the play comes to Blackfriars after the burning of the Globe, it therefore brings with it a sense of an ending, coupled with a vision of what was still to come, as the "King's Great Matter" in all its temporal, spatial, and acoustic complexity made its dramatic return. To paraphrase another line from Donne, theatres may be rather like graves, over time serving as "to more than one a bed," a dynamic of recurrent "re-placement" raises the question of what happens to such *in situ* heteroglossia once the physical structure itself disappears.[21] From the perspective of our own century, we might also wonder what happens when such a structure "reappears" by means of reconstruction, as in the Sam Wanamaker playhouse. Put another way, as Gaston Bachelard's asks: "how can rooms that have disappeared become abodes for an unforgettable past?"[22]

---

[21] John Donne, *John Donne's Poetry: Authoritative Texts, Criticism*, ed. Arthur L. Clements (New York: Norton, 1966), 37–38.

[22] Gaston Bachelard, *The Poetics of Space*, trans. Maria Jolas (Boston: Beacon, 1994), xxxvi.

One answer may lie in the archaeological approach of the Victorian stage. Take for example E. W. Godwin's 1864 assertion that the audience comes "to witness such a performance as will place us as nearly as possible as spectators of the original scene or of the thing represented, and this result is only possible where accuracy in every particular is assured."[23] Charles Keans's 1855 staging of *Henry VIII*, which included a printed text "that gives a long list of acknowledgements to contemporary documents and drawings," suggests something of how Blackfriars itself was effectively reconstituted in this fleshing out of an antecedent space by means of historically inflected dramatic representation.[24]

To complicate (or perhaps enrich is the better word) matters further, there is now another space in which these "strange echoes" resound with particular resonance—one that, though it is neither Katherine's nor Shakespeare's Blackfriars, nonetheless serves as yet another "sound house" of history and cultural memory. The Sam Wanamaker Playhouse's reconstruction of the original London playhouse (like that of the less proximal American Shakespeare Center) raises questions that lie beyond the scope of this article, though I would suggest in concluding that the difference between early modern repurposing and postmodern reconstruction may well be one of degree if not in kind. With each production of *Henry VIII*, Blackfriars rises again, and as the play reconstructs that space, that space in turn restages the dialogic interplay of long-lost speech with silence. As Bachelard reminds us, within that ephemeral yet resilient room, "not only our memories but the things we have forgotten are 'housed.'"[25] Heteroglossic silence seems to be "a thing we have forgotten" in our study of early modern culture, but when it is "housed" in this way, we are reminded that, like Caliban's island, Blackfriars is "full of noises," and some of them are silent.

Mercer University

---

[23] Quoted in Marvin Carlson, *Shattering Hamlet's Mirror: Theatre and Reality* (Ann Arbor: Univ. of Michigan Press, 2016), 95.

[24] Michael R. Booth, *Victorian Spectacular Theatre: 1850–1910* (New York: Routledge, 1981), 48–49.

[25] Bachelard, *The Poetics of Space*, xxxvii.

"What they are yet I know not": Speech, Silence, and Meaning in King Lear

John N. Wall

S HAKESPEARE'S *King Lear* ends oddly. It's not so much what happens that is odd, but what is said. Or, better, what isn't said. The play's action begins in division and winds its way to its inevitable consequences: lots of people die, and Edgar, Kent, and Albany are left to cope with the aftermath. We are used to lots of dead bodies on the stage at the end of Shakespeare's tragedies. And we are also accustomed to there being someone left behind to take over, to restore order, to say the last speech of the play. In *Lear*, Albany offers this part to Kent and Edgar, but Kent turns it down. Edgar does not reject the role, so we assume he accepts it, and so we reach at least a degree of return to stability at the end of *King Lear*. So far, so good. But what to me is odd is what happens next. Rather than state clearly his acceptance of authority, Edgar gives us his interpretation of the play's events. Describing the moment as a "sad time," Edgar calls for us to "Speak what we feel, not what we ought to say" (*Lear*, 5.3.325).[1]

That's a bit odd for a closing remark, and then things get even stranger because, though Edgar says this is a time to "Speak what we feel, not what we ought to say," he does not actually use the language of feeling at all. What we get instead at the end of *Lear* is the language of description, of interpretation, of expectation: Edgar says, "The oldest hath borne most; we that are young / Shall never see so much, nor live so long" (*Lear*, 5.3.327). And then, still without

---

[1] All quotations from Shakespeare's plays in this essay are from *The Riverside Shakespeare* (2nd ed.), ed. G. Blakemore Evans (Boston: Houghton Mifflin, 1997).

a word of feeling, Edgar and the rest of the cast, or at least those whose parts in the play have not been killed off, march off the stage to "a dead march," the slow beat of a drum. We in the audience are left with the bodies, and with the sound of the drum, and with the problem of what to make of what we have witnessed.

One way to describe the ending of *Lear* is to say that in this play the language runs out before the play is over. Indeed, it seems to me that over and over in this play, language runs out, or fails to account for, or proves inadequate to convince anyone that he or she can make sense of, what is going on. The play opens with this particular motif. Kent and Gloucester are discussing Lear's plans for retirement and the division of the kingdom. The plan they are discussing is one in which the kingdom is to be divided, but—in their understanding—the terms of this division should reflect Lear's attitudes toward his sons-in-law. Kent claims that he "thought the king had more affected the Duke of Albany than Cornwall." Gloucester agrees with Kent; he acknowledges that "It did always seem so to us." But now, he believes, "in the / division of the kingdom, it appears not which of / the dukes he values most" (*Lear*, 1.1.1–5). When Lear's plan is revealed to the court, and to us, Lear is of course talking about the daughters, demanding that the basis for the division lays with them, and with his evaluation of which of the three loves him most. Hence Lear's actual plan confounds Kent's and Gloucester's expectations. And, since the conversation between Kent and Gloucester has shaped our expectations as well, we join them in their surprise.

In these opening scenes, *King Lear* foregrounds the tendency of people to reach conclusions based on inadequate or out-of-date language. The play also demonstrates the human capacity to lie, for the speaker of language to misrepresent reality for the sake of some other end, such as getting a piece of one's inheritance early in life. After all, Goneril says that she loves her father "more than words can wield the matter" because it is a "love that makes breath poor, and speech unable" (*Lear*, 1.1.55–60). In spite of her claims, however, Goneril goes on to use a large number of words to declare her love, as does her sister Regan. Cordelia, his third daughter, echoes the literal meaning of Goneril's claims but not the result; finding that words are inadequate to compete with her sisters' outpouring of affection, she decides to "Love, and be silent" (*Lear*, 1.1.62).

Hence, the play demonstrates the limits of language's capacity to express what one believes to be true. Goneril's and Regan's speeches open up a space between the meaning of words that are spoken and the reality that lies (pun intended) behind them. Cordelia's speech opens up a space between her feelings and the capabilities of her language, or as she puts it, "I cannot heave / My heart into my mouth" (*Lear*, 1.1.91–92). Lying comes easy for some characters—Goneril, Regan, and Edmund, especially—while for others the necessity of truth-telling comes at a price. Lear's Fool, for example, suffers for his message and begs for release from his role, for instruction in how to avoid his task: "Prithee, nuncle, keep a schoolmaster that can teach / thy fool to lie: I would fain learn to lie" (*Lear*, 1.4.179–80).

After Lear's tightly scripted plan to distribute his kingdom and take early retirement from the responsibilities of monarchy falls into chaos, and into improvisation, Goneril and Regan join Gloucester and Edmund in seeking words to understand what has happened.[2] Goneril blames the turn of events on Lear's character; distancing herself from her own feelings, and from her relationship with her father, she takes what we might recognize as a distant, even clinical, stance:

> The best and soundest of his time hath been but
> rash; then must we look to receive from his age,
> not alone the imperfections of long-engraffed
> condition, but therewithal the unruly waywardness
> that infirm and choleric years bring with them.
> (*Lear*, 1.1.55–60)

Regan joins her in extrapolating in such terms from present events to future conditions; her father, she says, is likely to continue in his erratic behavior, in "such unconstant starts . . . as this of Kent's banishment." So they agree to "hit together" in their response, certain that "if our father carry authority with such dispositions . . . this last surrender of his will but offend us" (*Lear*, 1.1.295–306).

While his older daughters distance themselves from Lear, even as they benefit from the consequences of his actions, Kent's choice is

---

[2] Note the surprises that emerge in Lear's reopened negotiations with the duke of Burgundy and the king of France for Cordelia's hand in marriage.

to embrace Lear while confronting him with the reality of the situation. Kent chooses the language of relationships: He affirms "Royal Lear" as one whom he has "ever honour'd as my king, / Loved as my father, as my master follow'd, / As my great patron thought on in my prayers," yet now one to whom he must address in "plainness," as an "old man" who "stoops to folly," to "hideous rashness" (*Lear*, 1.1.139–51). Yet Lear remains in the world where division is the way to resolve difficulties; he threatens Kent in the language of archery, telling him that "The bow is bent and drawn, make from the shaft." But Kent says Lear should "Let it fall rather, though the fork invade / The region of my heart: be Kent unmannerly, / When Lear is mad." And so he is, telling Lear that while the king may "Kill . . . [his] physician," Kent will persist in venting "clamour from . . . [his] throat," by telling Lear "thou dost evil" (*Lear*, 1.1.143–66).

In spite of this harsh and confrontational scene, Kent, of course, is determined to continue his close relationship with Lear, and, banished by the king, returns to his service in disguise. With Kent's speech, however, the central motif of the play's opening action—division of the kingdom, which leads to division of Lear's family, then division of his court—now moves into the realm of language, and into the realm of the body. While Kent may describe Lear's threatened arrow as a "fork" that might invade Kent's heart, in the words of Lear's Fool, the king's actions become metaphors for acts of foolishness, enabling the Fool to promise that if Lear gives him an egg, he will give the king two crowns. When Lear questions his ability to do so, the Fool makes his case:

> Why, after I have cut the egg i' the middle, and eat
> up the meat, the two crowns of the egg. When thou
> clovest thy crown i' the middle, and gavest away
> both parts, thou borest thy ass on thy back o'er
> the dirt: thou hadst little wit in thy bald crown,
> when thou gavest thy golden one away. If I speak
> like myself in this, let him be whipped that first
> finds it so.
>
> (*Lear*, 1.4.158–65)

The Fool's comments continue to develop the circle of interpretations of Lear's behavior; like the response of Kent, the Fool's speeches develop further the motif of division but the need to speak such truths, brings the Fool no joy. As he points out to Lear the consequences of the king's decision to divide the kingdom, he distances himself, and Lear, and the audience as well, from the power of truth-speaking by breaking his message up into small bites, by varying them with elements of his comic repertoire, and by setting some of his speeches to music:

> Then they for sudden joy did weep,
> And I for sorrow sung,
> That such a king should play bo-peep,
> And go the fools among.
> (*Lear*, 1.4.175–8)

For the Fool, language enables the speaker to play with the truth, to vary styles of delivery so the changing styles distract from the power of the message while still delivering the message. In part because of the differences between his role and Kent's in Lear's court, the Fool gets by with telling Lear much the same message. The truth content of language is here disclosed to be limited by what one knows, but also by what one understands about what one knows. Beyond simply using language to misrepresent the truth, characters in this play also persist in resorting to verbal formulations of their understanding of the world of events.

As the action of the play divides families, kingdoms, and individuals, so it organizes characters into differing cognitive worlds. To Goneril, Lear's entourage consists of "Men so disorder'd, so debosh'd and bold, / That this our court, infected with their manners, Shows like a riotous inn . . . more like a tavern or a brothel / Than a graced palace." To Lear, however, they are "men of choice and rarest parts, / That all particulars of duty know, / And in the most exact regard support / The worships of their name" (*Lear*, 1.4.242–66).

Yet from within their own distinct understandings of events, their worlds are beginning to change. For Goneril, Lear is "of late transform[ed]" from what he rightly is (*Lear*, 1.4.221–2). From Lear's perspective, Goneril becomes for him a "Degenerate bastard," a "Detested kite" with "wolvish visage" (*Lear*, 1.4.253–54). In effect, Lear and his daughters enter a process of testing the power of their respective names, seeking to determine which of them can make his or her accounts of the world true or, at least, acceptable to those whom they expect to recognize who they are, to obey their commands and to share their worldview. Newly formed understandings lead to further division, to lack of comprehension, and to more questions than answers. Lear, for example, says he does not recognize the portrait of himself that Goneril is offering him: "Doth any here know me? This is not Lear." Looking around him to find anyone who understands that he is as he has been and is therefore worthy of being recognized and treated appropriately, he asks, "Doth Lear walk thus? speak thus? Where are his eyes? / . . . 'tis not so. / Who is it that can tell me who I am?" (Lear, 1.4.226–30).

Observations here lead not to answers but to more questions, examples of the ways in which in this play's action provides increasingly complex metaphors for understanding. The division of the kingdom soon reappears in metaphors of division that help describe a range of events, in both outward and inward settings, in both interactions among the characters and within their mental and emotional lives. Nowhere is this as clear, or as pervasive, as it is in the metaphor of seeing to describe knowing, or the act of knowing, that is, the act of understanding a situation as well as the act of observing it. At the beginning of the play, the king's plans for his kingdom had seemed to Gloucester to support one interpretation but now appears to support quite another one (*Lear*, 1.1.1–7). The act of seeing as knowing is made material in the maps that Lear uses to inform his elder daughters of what part of the kingdom they are to inherit. Yet avoiding the king's "sight" comes to define the terms of the banishment he imposes on Kent, even though Kent has argued that Lear should "see better . . . and let me still remain / The true blank of thine eye" (*Lear*, 1.1.158–59).

Like the word "nothing" in this play, which keeps recurring, in true protean fashion, long after Cordelia tells her father that she has nothing to say about her love for him, the word "sight" and the metaphor of seeing gets incorporated into speech after speech, then gets literalized once more in the actual blinding of Gloucester, which itself becomes another source of figurative language, from Lear's claim that he remembers Gloucester's (missing) eyes as a sign of Lear's madness, to his claim that one can "see how this world goes with no eyes," in response to Gloucester's comment that he sees "feelingly" (*Lear*, 4.6.149–51). Perhaps one of the most telling aspects of this play, of course, is in precisely the way in which the ending of Gloucester's sight becomes not the end, but the beginning, of a whole new realm of knowing.

Such interpretive gestures, such efforts to make sense of what is happening, are in *Lear* distributed across the cast rather than being confined to the speeches of a single Chorus or choric figure. Gloucester, for example, having watched the kingdom fall apart through Lear's bungling of his plan to have his daughters compete for his gift of land through verbal expressions of their love, then falls for Edmund's trick of a false letter from Edgar. Gloucester responds by applying an astrological worldview to make sense of it:

> These late eclipses in the sun and moon portend
> no good to us:
> . . . . .
> This villain of mine comes under the
> prediction; there's son against father: the king
> falls from bias of nature; there's father against
> child. We have seen the best of our time.
> (*Lear*, 1.2.103–12)

Gloucester's implicit determinism is echoed by Kent later in the play, when he argues that "It is the stars / The stars above us [that] govern our condition" (*Lear*, 4.3.45). But here, in act 1, before we have had a moment to consider the validity of Gloucester's mode of interpretation, and with it his understanding of causality, Edmund rejects it out of hand:

> This is the excellent foppery of the world, that,
> when we are sick in fortune we make guilty of our
> disasters the sun, the moon, and the stars: as
> if we were villains by necessity;
> . . . by an enforced obedience of
> planetary influence; and all that we are evil in,
> by a divine thrusting on: an admirable evasion
> of whoremaster man!
> (*Lear*, 1.2.118–27)

Edmund's rejection of external, celestial causality combines with an alternative and equally deterministic understanding of how we became who we are; he says, "I should have been that I am had

the maidenliest star in the firmament twinkled on my bastardizing" (*Lear*, 1.2.123–25). His affirmation of human responsibility for
one's actions displaces his father's astrological interpretation, which
Edmund dismisses as "an evasion of whoremaster man."

But events in the play also put such philosophical understandings of meaning to a variety of tests of their adequacy, of how well
they bear up under the press of events. Lear finds himself, as his
plans for retirement begin to unravel, losing the power of language
to describe or to create reality. Accustomed to having his commands
obeyed, he finds that Goneril and Regan pay no attention to his
demands that they keep the commitments they made to care for
him and his hundred knights. The result is a semantic debate about
the relationship between one's dress, one's entourage, and one's
basic humanity. His daughters claim that Lear does not need his
entourage:

> Hear me, my lord;
> What need you five and twenty, ten, or five,
> To follow in a house where twice so many
> Have a command to tend you?
> > (*Lear*, 2.4.260–63)

Lear, on the other hand, argues that one should

> reason not the need: our basest beggars
> Are in the poorest thing superfluous:
> Allow not nature more than nature needs,
> Man's life's as cheap as beast's: thou art a lady;
> If only to go warm were gorgeous,
> Why, nature needs not what thou gorgeous wear'st,
> Which scarcely keeps thee warm.
> > (*Lear*, 2.4.264–70)

Lear's proposal for a debate with Goneril and Regan about seman-
tics may well be a parody of his earlier command that they tell him
how much they love him; unfortunately, here, it serves as evidence
that Lear is losing—losing not only his knightly entourage and his
secure retirement, but also his capacity to imagine, to command,
even to speak:

> No, you unnatural hags,
> I will have such revenges on you both,

That all the world shall—I will do such things,—
What they are, yet I know not: but they shall be
The terrors of the earth.

(Lear, 2.4.278–82)

The point of Lear's comments would seem to be about how his failure of imagination and of language expresses his continuing loss of control of the situation he's in. At the same time, however, his remarks continue to open the space between language's capabilities to describe possibilities or to shape outcomes as well as space between characters and their capabilities for speaking.

Following the pattern set by Gloucester's comments on causality in the determining of human nature and the unfolding of events in history, which are followed by Edmund's comments on the same subject, Lear's comments on the value of clothing in his argument with Goneril and Regan are followed by contrasting comments, only this time they come from Lear himself. To his daughters, Lear says that if we "Allow not nature more than nature needs, / Man's life's as cheap as beast's" (Lear, 2.4.266–67).

There are at least two things worthy of note about how language works in this scene. First, Lear's initial use of clothing as a distinguishing mark of the human is part of an argument that distances him from Goneril and Regan; they wish to deprive him of things that are "more than nature needs," but he wants to keep them. In short, he is trying to hold on to people, relationships, and his personal authority. The power of the scene lies in the fact that as he is trying to hold on to things that inform his identity, that tell him he is still King Lear, we see those things slip away, dissolve into unknowing. "I will do such things," he says, "What they are, yet I know not."

Soon, as the play unfolds, Lear will use language about clothing again, and the kinds of clothing, and the relationship between the human and the animal again, only this time he uses them in responding to Edgar, who as Edgar has become "nothing," but, disguised as Tom a Bedlam, has become something quite different. Edgar is disguised, has taken "the basest and poorest shape / That ever penury, in contempt of man, / Brought near to beast" (Lear, 2.3.7–9). He describes his planned new identity in terms of outward appearance, good advice for the theater's costume designer, but also a reminder of the relationship between the appearances that language can create and the reality that will soon stand before us when we see the actor playing Edgar first appear in his new role.

Edgar promises to "grime with filth [my face]; / Blanket my loins: elf all my hair in knots; / And with presented nakedness outface / The winds and persecutions of the sky." His guide to acting this new role, his "proof and precedent," he learns from "Bedlam beggars," who, he says, become "horrid objects … with roaring voices, / [That] Strike in their numb'd and mortified bare arms / Pins, wooden pricks, nails, sprigs of rosemary." In Edgar's understanding, "poor Tom" is "something yet" when "as Edgar I nothing am" (*Lear*, 2.3.9–21).

We in the audience thus see Edgar plan and execute his own personal transformation. In other moments in the play we witness occasions in which similar transformations take place, yet they are often created from without, by other characters, rather than from within the authoring character. Edmund, for example, transforms Edgar from a loyal son to a potential parricide, at least from Gloucester's perspective; later in the play, he will perform a similar transformation for his father, making him appear to the duke of Cornwall to be a traitor, hence making himself into the duke of Gloucester. In passing moments, Goneril becomes for Lear no longer a loving daughter but a "Degenerate bastard," while Poor Tom becomes a "Noble philosopher" (*Lear*, 3.4.172).

Identity thus becomes a performance of appearances; one of the roles cast for the audience in this play is to be witness to these shifts in identity, to the relative character of identity as a category of thought, and to the power that language gives to the skillful user of language to create and sustain various appearances of identity. Creating new identities is a form of manipulation, but the other side of identity formation is seen in the several instances in which characters shift identities for the purpose of concealment, for protection, for restoration.

Edgar's description of the status of "Bedlam beggars" is constructed in contrast to his own birthright as the legitimate son of a wealthy and powerful man and heir to a dukedom; in contrast, he now aspires to be both "basest" and "poorest." Yet, in a scene in which questions of what language can communicate multiply extravagantly, Edgar-as-Tom provokes in Lear a momentary relief from the raging mind that embraces the ravages of the storm. Lear interprets Edgar/Tom in the terms of his own experience, identifying with Tom and seeing him as someone who must also share Lear's fate of being someone abused by his daughters. Then, in the midst of this cognitive muddle, Lear says something that is either an extension of Lear's confusion or a moment of remarkable clarity:

> Thou wert better in thy grave than to answer
> with thy uncovered body this extremity of the skies.
> Is man no more than this? Consider him well.
>
> . . . . .
>
> Thou art the thing itself:
> unaccommodated man is no more but such a poor bare,
> forked animal as thou art.
>
> (*Lear*, 3.4.101–8)

Based on Lear's recognition of Tom / Edgar as "the thing itself," the king responds, "Off, off, you lendings! / come unbutton here" (*Lear*, 3.4.108–9). Lear is moving toward Edgar rather than arguing with him, responding to Edgar's situation not with further argument or definition or description, but with action, with removal of his own clothing, to join Tom in his vulnerability before the raging storm, and also to shield Tom from those elements.

This issue of the adequacy of language to deal with influencing events or to account for how things turn out reaches its most critical moment at the beginning of act 4 when Edgar, having survived his night of performing the role of Tom a' Bedlam while extremely underdressed for the part, recognizes that the dawn has come and he is still alive and free. So he boasts, "To be worst, / The lowest and most dejected thing of fortune" is not so bad after all, because it "still stands" in hope, "lives not in fear." So, he says, "Welcome, then, / Thou unsubstantial air that I embrace. / The wretch that thou has blown unto the worst / Owes nothing to thy blasts." But then he sees his father, the duke of Gloucester, blind, wretched, stumbling, despairing, beyond comfort, rejecting human companionship, afraid his company will bring harm to people who seek to help him. And Edgar says "Who is't can say, 'I am at the worst'? / I am worse than e'er I was." / And worse I may be yet; the worst is not / So long as we can say, 'This is the worst'" (*Lear*, 4.1.2–25).

Edgar says, in effect, that so long as we have language, so long as we can find words to describe what is happening, things are not as bad as they can get. Language distances us from experience, says Edgar, even while it enables us to communicate whatever under-standing we might make of our experience. "The worst is not yet," says Edgar, so long as we can say, "This is the worst." This sepa-ration between words and feeling is also performed for us at the play's darkest emotional moment. In act 5, of course, Lear enters "with Cordelia dead in his arms," and, having lost the possibility of words to express his grief, is left only with howling. Lear says, "Howl, howl, howl," clearly here not as dialogue, but as stage direc-tion (*Lear*, 5.4.101–8). The death of one's child is the worst, and especially here, when the child who dies has transformed in Lear's understanding from being one "adopted to [Lear's] hate" (*Lear*, 1.1.101) to becoming one to whom he must kneel and beg forgive-ness (Lear, 4.8.82); so what is called for here *is* howling, a sound from the depth of our humanity, from our bestial depths, from the depths of our being a "poor, bare, forked animal" (*Lear*, 3.4.105–7), crying out from the very experience of despair, and disappointment, and sorrow, and grief.

In the midst of all this linguistic uncertainty, of all the variet-ies of meaning, of all the conflicts of interpretation, *Lear* still offers us compensatory moments. These moments come, not in efforts to understand what is happening, but in the context of interactions between characters who care deeply for one another. There is the role of the Fool, who finds ways to speak truth through word-game and song. There are the self-sacrificial roles of Kent and Edgar, who literally give up themselves by taking on disguises, deliberately lying about who they are and how they understand the world. Kent, of course, does this to remain close to Lear; Edgar does it to escape his father's wrath over the false charges that Edmund lodges against Edgar. There is the moment we have already mentioned, when Lear recognizes in Edgar / Tom a Bedlam a sign of their common humanity.

These moments run counter to the play's main narrative energy, which runs toward division, separation, fragmentation, and death. Set in motion by Lear's initial act of dividing the kingdom among his daughters, this trajectory plays itself out in actions—in the sepa-rations of Lear, Cordelia, and Kent; of Gloucester and Edgar; of Lear, Goneril, and Regan; of Gloucester, Goneril, and Regan; of Cornwall and Albany; of Albany and Goneril; and, ultimately, of

Goneril and Regan, who die competing with each other for the affections of Edmund. This progressive divisiveness is seen in the language of the play, as it moves from the Fool's account of events in terms of the division of an egg into two crowns to Edgar's claim that had his father not been "aught but gossamer, feathers, air," he would have shattered like an egg (*Lear*, 4.5.49–50). Goneril's understanding of the effects of hosting Lear and his entourage is that his presence is setting "us all at odds" (*Lear*, 1.3.4); Gloucester's "old heart is crack'd, it's crack'd!" (*Lear*, 2.1.90) by supposed news of Edgar's treachery; Edmund decides to persevere in "loyalty" to the new regime rather than to his father, even though "the conflict be sore between that and my blood" (*Lear*, 3.5.19–22). By the end of the play, of course, Edmund is debating with himself which of Lear's daughters he should "take," and considering a wide range of possibilities: "Both? One? Or neither?" (*Lear*, 5.1.57–58).

The central action of the play is thus about the breaking of traditional bonds and customs of social order. Lear disrupts the traditional process of transferring authority from one generation to the next by abdicating his responsibility to maintain, and to exercise, the role of king before he has the authority to do so in a hereditary monarchy. The result is a series of rebellions by the younger generation against their parents, seen most dramatically in the way Edmund becomes duke of Gloucester, not by inheritance but by betrayal, which ultimately leads to Goneril's and Regan's abdicating their vows to their husbands and their responsibilities to each other as co-monarchs. Contesting against social custom, these characters act increasingly in terms of their own understandings of their own self-interest rather than in terms of any sense of obligation to or responsibility for the larger social order.

Eventually, the play's characters loosely divide into two larger groups: those hostile to Lear and those loyal to Edmund. The language of description of those hostile to Lear also follows a progress in which Goneril, Regan, Edmund and their allies are increasingly identified as bestial, as less than human. Lear starts this off by reframing Cordelia as "a stranger to [his] heart" (*Lear*, 1.1.115) and by bastardizing Goneril. Soon, Gloucester is, to Regan, an "Ingrateful fox" and "filthy traitor" (*Lear*, 2.7.28, 32), while, to Gloucester, Goneril has "boarish fangs" (*Lear*, 3.8.57), while, to Goneril, her husband Albany exhibits "cowish terror" (*Lear*, 4.2.11). To Albany,

Goneril and Regan have become "Tigers, not daughters" and Goneril has become "a fiend" (*Lear*, 4.2.40, 60). To Kent, they are "dog-hearted daughters" (*Lear*, 4.3.45). To Edmund, Goneril's and Regan's desire for him, and jealousy of each other, is as the behavior of "the adder" (*Lear*, 5.1.57–58). To Edgar, Edmund becomes a "toad-spotted traitor" (*Lear*, 5.1.57–58). And so forth.

On the other hand, the characters who remain loyal to Lear gradually become described in terms of lightness, of flight, of airiness. As we have seen, Edgar says of his father that his survival of a (supposed) fall from the Cliffs of Dover was because he was "gossamer, feathers, air" (*Lear*, 4.6.50). Of Cordelia, Lear says that she is "a spirit," "a soul in bliss" (*Lear*, 4.7.45, 48) and, according to a gentleman, she "redeems nature from the general curse" (*Lear*, 4.6.206). These characters increasingly become involved in scenes in which characters are brought back together, reconciled to each other. As the play proceeds, these moments become increasingly theatrical, in the sense that they act out the powers of the imagination to "give to aery nothingness a local habitation and a name" (*MSND*, 5.1.16–17).

Edgar creates for Gloucester a therapeutic process for restoration, for role-play, for imaginative creation of place and time, for the power of invention and transformation in order to bring Gloucester from his despairing belief that we are "to the gods as flies to wanton boys / They kill us for their sport" into a new place where he can promise to "bear / Affliction till it do cry out itself / 'Enough, enough'" (*Lear*, 4.5.75–77). And, if Edgar is to be believed, this transformative process continues, until Edgar reveals himself to his father.

> I ask'd his blessing, and from first to last
> Told him my pilgrimage: but his flaw'd heart,
> 'Twixt two extremes of passion, joy and grief,
> Burst smilingly.
> (*Lear*, 5.3.196–200)

There is also, in Shakespeare's dramatization of Lear's madness, an extended exploration of the king's effort to realize once more his authority, that he is "every inch a king," through drawing conclusions—"A man may see how this world goes with no eyes" (*Lear*, 4.6.165)—through giving orders—"Let copulation thrive"—and by seeking to exercise power—"Give me an ounce of civet, / good apothecary, to sweeten my imagination: / there's money for thee" (*Lear*, 4.6.132–46) We recognize, in Lear's speeches in conversation with Gloucester, the world we knew from the earlier parts of the play, yet a world turned upside down, a world in which Lear remembers correctly "When the rain came to / wet me once, and the wind to make me chatter; when / the thunder would not peace at my bidding." But Lear still believes that "Gloucester's bastard son / Was kinder to his father than my daughters / Got 'tween the lawful sheets" (*Lear*, 4.6.96–130).

Yet with this recognition comes a more humbling awareness. In act 2, Lear values clothing as a sign of authority, even of one's humanness, since if one allows "not nature more than nature needs, / Man's life's as cheap as beasts" (*Lear*, 2.4.266–68); in act 3, Edgar's lack of clothing reveals to Lear "the thing itself," reveals "unaccommodated man" as "but a poor, bare, forked animal" (*Lear*, 3.4.106–7); now he takes that insight back up the social hierarchy, recognizing that the appearance of rank and privilege protects those at the top of society from the consequences of their actions while the poor are made all the more vulnerable by their bareness:

> Through tattered clothes great vices do appear;
> Robes and furred gowns hide all. Plate sin with gold,
> And the strong lance of justice hurtless breaks.
> Arm it in rags, a pigmy's straw does pierce it.
>
> (*Lear*, 4.6.164–67)

Lear's journey through the second half of this play mirrors that of Gloucester, so it is appropriate that Edgar is the companion of both, guiding the one from despair to stoic acceptance and also noting in the other that "matter and impertinency [are] mix'd, / Reason in madness!" (*Lear*, 4.6.174–75). Although it takes Lear more stage-time than it takes Gloucester to make it from the world of delusion and despair to a world of renewed clarity of understanding, Gloucester's journey is hastened by, and dependent on, his son Edgar's mastery of a therapeutic stagecraft. Lear's transition from madness to a renewed ability to recognize seems to hinge ultimately on his being reunited with his daughter Cordelia, in that powerful scene when they meet at last and something comes of it:

Pray, do not mock me:
I am a very foolish fond old man,
Fourscore and upward, not an hour more nor less;
And, to deal plainly, I fear I am not in my perfect mind.
Methinks I should know you, and know this man;
Yet I am doubtful . . . Do not laugh at me;
For, as I am a man, I think this lady
To be my child Cordelia.

(*Lear*, 4.7.58–69)

Lear's vision of their future together, once the French army has lost the battle against the forces of Goneril, Regan, and Edmund, is to propose that they spend their days transforming the world through the powers of their imaginations. Indeed, the play marks the recovery of Lear precisely in Lear's recovery of his capabilities of the imagination. Earlier, he could not imagine the awful things he planned for Goneril and Regan; now he easily imagines the richness of a life with Cordelia, even one confined to a cell:

We two alone will sing like birds i' the cage:
When thou dost ask me blessing, I'll kneel down,
And ask of thee forgiveness: so we'll live,
And pray, and sing, and tell old tales, and hear poor rogues
Talk of court news; and we'll talk with them too,
Who loses and who wins; who's in, who's out;
And take upon's the mystery of things.

(*Lear*, 5.3.9–16)

But, of course, the forces Lear has unleashed by trying to retire from ruling the kingdom ultimately overwhelm even Lear's restored imaginative capabilities. Indeed, in *Lear*, the events of the play expose for us both the incessant human effort to see, to understand, to articulate what is happening, but also the limits on that very effort to see clearly and articulate what is universally true. What happens next after one character or another offers us meaning often turns inside out whatever meaning has been made of what has gone before. How appropriate, therefore, that the play ends not with words but with sound, a sound that in its repetitiveness is what finally brings the play to a close—that, and the conventions of theater that any play must end in some specific time and place, restoring in its own experiential way the order of things.

So that it is the play we are left with—not the words of the play, exactly, but the play performed, with us in the audience, or, better said, our experience of the play performed, so that we share with the characters onstage the events we have seen and the conversations about those events we have overheard. Parts of what we experience are the responses to these events exhibited by the characters, both in verbal and in nonverbal forms. We may find their responses adequate, or not; we do have—and the characters do not—the chance for second thoughts, the chance to reach our own conclusions, the chance to relive the events of the play itself. I, personally, am partial to Edgar's belief that "men must endure our going hence even as our coming hither. / The ripeness is all." But the best the play can come to affirming that is to have Gloucester say, "And that's true, too" (*Lear*, 5.2.9–11).

So the words are often hollow, partial, or inadequate to the situation. But we do have a play in which the most affecting moments are the moments that come not in characters' reflections in language, but in the events in which characters recognize each other by connecting emotionally and cognitively with each other. And we have the drum; consider for a moment the text of *Lear* as prologue, preparing us for the drum, the dead march that closes the play. This play reminds us of the points at which theater and ritual overlap, or, to put it another way, to revisit the points at which the ancient links between theater and ritual, between play and liturgy, become visible again. The places that underlie Aristotle's claim that theater, especially tragic theater, is therapeutic because it enables us to experience "incidents arousing pity and fear, wherewith to accomplish a catharsis of these emotions."[3] In the serious matters of human life, it is not so much the statements of belief or understandings of the situation that matter, but, this play suggests, the companionship.

North Carolina State University

---

[3] Aristotle, *Poetics*, trans. Ingram Bywater, book 6, https://www.authorama.com/the-poetics-7.html.

Shakespearean Epiphany

Robert Lanier Reid

"That is why the theatre, for which nothing exists except the epiphanic, is so central an epitome of life."

—Northrop Frye[1]

S HAKESPEARE'S most compelling play begins with a haunting, a command from below stage, "Swear!" as the prince pleads, "Rest, rest, perturbed spirit!" The affronted ghost, furiously disclosing a murder that poisons familial and communal bonds, rouses the depths of human nature, but not so deep as other scenes, in *Hamlet* and in other plays, of genuine epiphany, which intimate the fullness and destiny of human nature. Are such scenes entirely secular, as some critics insist, or do they bear a supernatural energy and a sacral purpose? In nearly forty plays over more than twenty years, does the spiritual depth charge intensify, and does Shakespeare's religious profile become more overt? Most epiphanies, of course, are positive, life-affirming and faith restoring; they fix people's brokenness, notably in the romances; but are there negative

---

[1] Northrop Frye, *Northrop Frye's Notebooks and Lectures on the Bible and Other Religious Texts*, ed. Robert D. Denham, in *Collected Works* (Toronto: Univ. of Toronto Press, 2003), 13:323. Elsewhere Frye insists that his main critical method is not so much archetypal as epiphanic. Frye, *The "Third Book" Notebooks of Northrop Frye, 1964–1972*, ed. Michael Dolzani, in *Collected Works*, 9:52. For my earlier views of this topic, see R. L. Reid, "Epiphanal Encounters in Shakespearean Dramaturgy," *Comparative Drama* 32, no. 4 (1998–99): 518–40; revised in *Shakespeare's Tragic Form: Spirit in the Wheel* (Newark: Univ. of Delaware Press; London: Associated Univ. Presses, 2000), 69–88; and further revised in *Renaissance Psychologies: Spenser and Shakespeare* (Manchester: Manchester Univ. Press, 2017), 239–51.

epiphanies, scenes of chaos, horror, desolation, showing deep malice in human nature and implying an absent or cruel God? Finally, how does Shakespeare manage this potent device in plotting a play? Is it a single revelation, like the discovery scene of Greek tragedy, or do Shakespeare's plays present an incremental series of epiphanies, each placed at the center of a passional cycle, and together building to a soul shaking revelation?

For Christians, epiphany is a major event, showing God among us. Epiphany Day (January 6), the twelfth day of Christmastide, celebrates the magi's visit to a baby who incarnated God as an earthly being. Scholars have compared this to the divine showings of other cultures. We are charmed by the Greek hero Odysseus meeting his crafty guardian Athena and by the dutiful Roman hero Aeneas meeting his doting mother Venus. In Greek tragedies we admire Apollo and Athena as rational arbiters who can appease the vengeful Furies, and show King Oedipus his proud errancy.[2] The *Bhagavad-Gita's* divine encounters are more complex and awe-inspiring: Krishna's profound sensual allure of Gopi women gives way in wartime to Prince Arjuna's dismay at Krishna's horrific totality, seeing many friends and admired teachers gored on the god's tusks.[3] As we shall see, Shakespeare's showings resemble Hinduism's in worldly prolixity and in facing annihilative darkness. But does he differ, intimating something more?

Quite distinct is the Christian epiphany. Joseph Campbell's sweeping analysis of world mythologies provides no other example with the historicity and wonder of the gospel story, leading to Margery Kempe's endless sobbing in Jerusalem and Dante's rapture at the vision of Paradise.[4] What then was Shakespeare's view of his staged

---

[2] After Apollo gives an ineffective patriarchal defense of Orestes for slaying his mother, the androgynous Athena brings resolution by affirming the Furies' passion, thereby transforming them into Eumenides ("kindly ones") and enabling the use of trial by jury. For this lovely insight, I am obliged to my friend Stephen Kennamer.

[3] See "The Song of the Lord," in *Mahabharata: A Modern Retelling*, trans. Carole Satyamurti (New York: Norton, 2015), 6:395–420.

[4] For debate on the historical Jesus, see Huston Smith, *The World's Religions* (New York: Harper Collins, 1991), 317–46; Marcus Borg, *Jesus: A New Vision* (San Francisco: Harper & Row, 1988); Karen Armstrong, *A History of God: The 4000-Year Quest of Judaism, Christianity, and Islam* (New York: Ballantine, 1993). 79–88.

epiphanies? Like the Medieval mystery plays he saw as a child, his art is both deeply spiritual and playfully ironic, but always with an under-tow of questioning. During several centuries of scientific Enlight-enment, the questioning expands and gains a sharp edge: Voltaire's barbed satire, Austen's sensible disillusion, Joyce's ironic materialism, and now the shifting alternative realities of the disunited states of Trump's America. Is epiphany still possible on a cracking planet?

What exactly is epiphany? For anyone, whether in the era from Augustine to Dante, or from Shakespeare to the present, the wit-nessing of God occurs in narrowing fields of vision. Beyond most of us is *the direct vision of God*, the *summum bonum* of seeing God face to face. How happy, Jesus says, are those whose hearts are pure, for they shall see God.[5] Nested inside that overwhelming encounter is *the humbler vision of God as Jesus*, specially manifested in the nativity, but also in the baptism, transfiguration, crucifixion, and the resur-rection, as well as in all the daily encounters: "Anyone who has seen me has seen the Father."[6] To assist the impure, God comes to us. Some, however, say that Jesus, like the Creator-God, is now absent, despite Jesus's claim of identity with the poor and needy who are always with us. So nested inside the showing of Jesus is *a meeting with any good person*, someone like Mother Teresa, clearly "made in God's image," sharing God's light with the needy as a loving par-ent holds a child. Last is *a vision of one's own Godliness*, drawn out by godly others who help us recall our own best self by bringing a mutual indwelling of souls by epiphanies of love. So we keep in mind these declensions of epiphany—seeing God, seeing God as

---

[5] Does the "pure heart" needed for full epiphany imply chastity or char-ity? Chaste separation from worldliness or loving service to others? (Or, more likely, both?) K. E. Kirk in *The Vision of God: The Christian Doctrine of the Summum Bonum* (New York: Harper & Row, 1966) decries rigorism as he surveys gospel and monastic quests for purity of heart to gain the vision. Bernard McGinn in *The Presence of God: A History of Western Christian Mysticism* (New York: Crossroads, 1991–present; 6 vols. completed) gives a remarkably detailed history and analysis of mystic experience. Karen Arm-strong, *A History of God*, influenced by Frazier's *Golden Bough* and Joseph Campbell's *The Masks of God* but personalizing and moving beyond them, provocatively compares the diverse notions of God in major religions.

[6] I.e., sees the One who begot me (John 14:9; cf. 1:18, 5:37, 6:46, 8:38, 10:22–38, 17:22–23, 20:29).

Jesus, seeing Jesus in a saintly person, seeing ourselves as possible saints. These entwined cycles of vision might help us understand the ranging complexity of epiphanic moments in Shakespeare's plays.

Three astute critics, Robert Langbaum, Ashton Nichols, and Martin Bidney have discussed "modern epiphany." Counteracting Enlightened skepticism, which oddly they do not explore as the constrictive *cause* of spiritual reaction, they see this new epiphany bursting forth in Romantic poetry, notably Wordsworth's overflow of powerful feelings that glory in the natural world: "spots of time" like the "host of golden daffodils" enjoyed with friends like Dorothy and Coleridge.[7] All three critics explain this new epiphany as "the romantic substitute for religion."[8] They stress Wordsworth's pantheism, not his ode to immortality, and they marginalize Blake's mystic vision. They fast-forward to James Joyce's skeptical apostasy, his redefining epiphany as a radiance which appears accidentally in common, vulgar things with no connection to God. Such materialist vision, these critics say, is pervasive in novels of Joyce, Woolf, Proust, Faulkner, in the poems of Eliot, Browning, Stevens, Yeats—indeed in most modern literature. Where committed religious vision occurs—for example, the poems of Hopkins, and Eliot's late work—it is not fully evaluated as such but is subordinated to the presumed dominance of a materialist, ego-psychological nature vision. Quite overlooked is the fuller epiphany, focused on God and on humankind as God's image, that is the hidden subtext in much modern literature, including Joyce.[9] For

---

[7] Robert Langbaum, *The Word from Below: Essays on Modern Literature and Culture* (Madison: Univ. of Wisconsin Press, 1987); *The Mysteries of Identity: A Theme in Modern Literature* (Chicago: Univ. of Chicago Press, 1983); Ashton Nichols, *The Poetics of Epiphany: Nineteenth-Century Origins of the Modern Literary Moment* (Tuscaloosa: Univ. of Alabama Press, 1987); Martin Bidney, *Patterns of Epiphany: From Wordsworth to Tolstoy, Pater, and Barrett Browning* (Carbondale: Southern Illinois Univ. Press, 1997).

[8] Langbaum, *The Word from Below*, 56. See M. H. Abrams, *Natural Supernaturalism: Tradition and Revolution in Romantic Literature* (New York: Norton, 1971), 97–140.

[9] Irene Hendry, "Joyce's Epiphanies," in *James Joyce: Two Decades of Criticism*, ed. Sean Givens (New York: Vanguard Press, 1948, 1963), 27–46; Robert Scholes, "Joyce and the Epiphany," *Sewanee Review* 72, no. 1 (1964): 65–77; Richard Ellman, *James Joyce* (New York: Oxford Univ. Press, 1965), 87–89 passim; Abrams, *Natural Supernaturalism*, 421–22, 528n23, 529n25.

these critics, however, modern epiphany is just, to use the words of E. E. Cummings, a "little lame balloon-man whistling far and wee."[10]

What then of Shakespeare's plays: do they reenact the medieval quest for godly vision, or do they focus only on Nature's glory, partly allaying psyche's anxious coil in a mortal body?[11] Shakespeare illuminates human nature in an open ground between these extremes. His epiphany evolves in radical leaps, disclosing human visions of Godliness in the following eight ways.

1) Shakespeare's main epiphanic insight is *the vision of oneself as another*.[12] *The Comedy of Errors* presents it early on. We see that the twinship is a complementary doubling, with one twin a restless wanderer and the other a frustrated homebody, so the concluding epiphany resolves that psychic division. But we sense a deeper message: the reunion of twins implies a universal siblinghood, laying the basis for the divine vision of epiphany: "Love God entirely, and love your neighbor as yourself."[13] In *The Comedy of Errors* such deep bonding is implied in the oceanic image used by the wandering twin, then by the other twin's wife, to show a yearning for consummate relationship:

> Antipholus S: I to the world am like a drop of water
> That in the ocean seeks another drop,
> Who, falling there to find his fellow forth,
> Unseen, inquisitive, confounds himself;

---

[10] For this oblique reference to the god Pan, see E. E. Cummings, part 1 of "Chansons Innocentes" from *Tulips and Chimneys* (1922), in *Complete Poems, 1910–1962*, vol. 1 (London: Granada, 1981), 27.

[11] On Shakespearean epiphany via revelatory scenes in the mystery plays, see T. G. Bishop, *Shakespeare and the Theater of Wonder* (Cambridge: Cambridge Univ. Press, 1996).

[12] See Paul Ricoeur, *Oneself as Another* (Chicago: Univ. of Chicago Press, 1995).

[13] The "great commandment" (Deut. 6:4–5) focuses entirely on loving God. Jesus adds another, "like unto it," which in the Torah (Lev. 19:18) encourages solidarity among the chosen people, but Jesus makes it universal. Is this second commandment, "love others as oneself," essential to fulfilling the first, "love God entirely"? (Does it show the "pure heart" that enables one to "see God"—that is, seeing God in others, especially in the poor and needy?).

> So I, to find a mother and a brother,
> In quest of them, unhappy, lose myself.

Adriana: How comes it now, my husband, O, how comes it,
           That thou art then estranged from thyself?
           Thyself, I call it, being strange to me
           That, undividable, incorporate,
           Am better than thy dear self's better part.
           Ah, do not tear away thyself from me
           For know, my love, as easy mayst thou fall
           A drop of water in the breaking gulf,
           And take unmingled thence that drop again
           Without addition or diminishing,
           As take from me thyself and not me too."
                           (*CE* 1.2.35–40; 2.2.118–28).[14]

This metaphor, which is nowhere in Shakespeare's source, implicitly exalts the desire for deep bonding by contextualizing it in the mystic ocean of Being which is God. *Twelfth Night* elaborates this twinship as male and female, more fully encompassing human identity in transgendered epiphany. In other plays of his middle period, Shakespeare uses cross-dressed disguise and regal self-fashioning—Hal, Portia, Rosalind—to show the relational epiphany as, in part, personally engineered and enacted. In sum, in every play the essential action is initiated, magnified, and finally resolved by revelatory disclosure of a mirroring other.

2) Deepening the vision of oneself as another is *the epiphany of romantic love.* Juliet and Romeo seem at first sight to see God in each other, and of course speak a perfect sonnet together to consummate their epiphany which grows as they resist feuds, forgive each other's mistakes, and commit a mutual love-death. A more mature love-epiphany occurs in *Othello* when in act 1 a racially mixed couple convince us and the Venetian court of their genuine affection, developed by patient discourse, not love at first sight (1.3.78–303). Though Iago's clever malice far exceeds the evil of the earlier tragedy, it ultimately heightens the wonder, for despite Othello's errancy, Desdemona holds fast to the epiphany of her beloved as godlike,

---

[14] Shakespeare quotations are taken from *The Complete Works of Shakespeare*, updated 7th ed., ed. David Bevington (New York: Pearson/Longman, 2013).

finally drawing both Othello and even skeptical Emilia into her vision of holiness.

3) Matching the love epiphany is *the epiphany of heroic valor*, inspired by deep bonds with family and nation: the Talbots' loyal self-sacrificing bravery in *1 Henry VI* (4.5–4.7), Othello and Desdemona's mutual warriorhood in *Othello* (2.1.181), and Henry V rousing his soldiers to courageous brotherhood on Crispin's Day in *Henry V* (4.3.18–67). But increasingly in Shakespeare's portrayal of great warriors—Hotspur, Achilles, Macbeth, Coriolanus—the skilled violence fosters a self-preening detachment, making Coriolanus question familial and communal bonds, yearning to be an "author of himself" who "knew no other kin" (*Cor* 5.3.34–37).[15]

4) Shakespeare's most influential vision is *the epiphany of a perfect man*.[16] Hamlet—a marvel of courtly polish, soldierly courage, and philosophic insight—greatly advances the earlier experiment with Henry V, especially by embroiling the gifted prince so deeply in tragedy that he ardently questions the human capacity for perfection. But distraction by the vengeful spirit and ongoing courtly treachery leads Hamlet to restage primal evil and to rebuff Ophelia's affection, minimizing her being and utterly missing her passionate devastation, thus distorting and avoiding full epiphany, except indirectly by means of a friendly gravedigger and Horatio.

5) Equally magnificent and truncated is Shakespeare's *epiphany of a perfect woman*, inspiring man and measuring his imperfection, though not fully asserting her own intellect and moral character.[17] Such a conceit of womanly perfection informs the mythic grandeur of Titania and Cleopatra, and it gains sacral impact in Desde-

---

[15] Patriotic militancy, partly idealized by Shakespeare until its ambivalent portrayal in the second *Henriad*, thereafter descends into horrors. Cf. Roy Battenhouse, "*Henry V* in the Light of Erasmus," *Shakespeare Studies* 17 (1985): 77–88; H. C. Goddard, *The Meaning of Shakespeare* (Chicago: Univ. of Chicago Press, 1985), 1:217–60.

[16] Hamlet, combining aspects of Castiglione's courtier, Machiavelli's prince, and More's self-effacing utopian ruler, draws the intelligentsia of every nation into his spell. See William Kerrigan, *Hamlet's Perfection* (Baltimore: Johns Hopkins Univ. Press, 1996); Harold Bloom, *Hamlet: Poem Unlimited* (New York: Riverhead Books, 2004).

[17] See Armstrong, *A History of God*, 234–35, 249, et passim, on female aspects of God.

mona, Cordelia, Hermione, and Miranda. And yet their philosophic consciousness is repeatedly silenced by repression, exile, or sleep. Not one drawing aside to confront spirit-powers or to question being and nothingness, despite the magnification of their intellective power by deep affection.

Three other Shakespearean epiphanies involve not just a single soul such as the twin, lover, warrior, philosophic man, sapient woman, but broad fields of communal and metaphysical being.

6) Extremely important is *the political epiphany of an ideal monarch as an image of God, inspiring a godly commonwealth.*[18] This epiphany is travestied in the first *Henriad*, then attains much success in the second *Henriad*, but is severely tested in the two great tragedies, *Macbeth* and *King Lear*, as well as in the final romances, *The Winter's Tale* and *The Tempest*. A keynote of the collective epiphany is the "ensemble scene" showing a royal ruler or parody-ruler enmeshed in a crowd of comrades or enemies: Bottom performing with the rustics, Hal and Falstaff with the tavern-dwellers, Hamlet dueling, and Cleopatra's death amid an entourage of devotees and rivals. In *King Lear* this vision of an embattled leader is almost constant: the opening ritual, the mad scenes, the apocalyptic ending. As in opera, major and minor characters blend their different voice registers and states of being into a dynamic exchange that reveals humankind's symphonic complexity.[19]

7) Most puzzling of Shakespeare's transformative visions is *the beast epiphany*, drawing on Apuleius's *Golden Ass* and Ovid's *Metamorphoses*, but also on Erasmus's *In Praise of Folly* and the biblical merkavah vision. The human-divine encounter assumes animal forms—first as hilarious parody: Bottom as ass enjoys epiphanic intimacy with an immortal fairy; and Falstaff as a "roasted

---

[18] E.g., Israel's King David and King Solomon, England's Queen Elizabeth and Queen Victoria. See Ernst Kantorowicz, *The King's Two Bodies: A Study in Medieval Political Theology* (Princeton, NJ: Princeton Univ. Press, 1957); Regina Schultz, *The Body of the Queen: Gender and Rule in the Courtly World, 1500–2000* (New York: Berghahn Books, 2014).

[19] This opera analogue for *King Lear* is drawn from W. H. Auden's celebrated *Lectures on Shakespeare*, ed. Arthur Kirsch (Princeton, NJ: Princeton Univ. Press, 2000), 220, 309–10, 321. Alas that Verdi never realized his ardent wish to compose an opera of *King Lear*.

Manningford ox with the pudding in his belly" (*1HIV* 2.4.447–48) is the scapegoat for all uncontrollable appetites. In the darkest tragedies the beastliness turns serious as Macbeth's witches mix human and animal body bits into their cauldron and as Lear strips off his clothes to identify with the beggar as "a poor bare forked animal." In Shakespeare's valedictory epiphany, *The Tempest*, the bestial Caliban is a central component.[20]

8) Most important and hardest to comprehend is the enormous scope of ***negative epiphany***. Deity may seem clearest in those generous-spirited heroes who are blessed with sunlike being, but do we also glimpse divinity in horrific kenotic scenes: amputated tongueless Lavinia, Malvolio and Shylock baited, Gloucester blinded, Cordelia hanged, tyrants exulting in cruelty?[21] Why taunt us with such harrowing scenes? The provocative science show *Cosmos* in its third episode shows the supreme energy force not as the gravitational mass of giant planets, nor as the light of dazzling suns, but rather as a vast black hole, sucking everything into itself. It recalls Hegel's "portentous power of the negative,"[22] Keats's notion of Shakespeare's "negative capability," and mystics like John of the Cross finding God in a "dark night of the soul."[23]

We must keep in mind all these modes of epiphany as a basis for our last consideration: how does Shakespeare maximize epiphany's power by its placement and function in a play? Aristotle in his *Poetics* explains the vital role of a single discovery scene in Greek tragedy. In contrast, Shakespeare in play after play composes an

---

[20] As Frank Kermode elaborately explains in his introduction to Shakespeare's *The Tempest*, ed. Frank Kermode (London and New York: Methuen, 1964), xxxiv–xliii.

[21] On demonic epiphany (the *visio malefica*, the *tour abolie*), see Northrop Frye, *Anatomy of Criticism* (Princeton, NJ: Princeton Univ. Press, 1957), 223, 238–39.

[22] "Preface to the Phenomenology of Mind," *Hegel Selections*, ed. J. Loewenberg (New York: Charles Scribner's Sons, 1929), 28–29: "it is the energy of thought, of pure ego. . . . It only wins to its truth when it finds itself in utter desolation; . . . mind is this power only by looking the negative in the face and dwelling with it."

[23] John Keats, *The Complete Poetical Works and Letters of John Keats, Cambridge Edition*, ed. Horace E. Scudder (Boston: Houghton, Mifflin and Company, 1899), 277.

incremental series of such turning-points, most brilliantly in *King Lear*, his greatest and most complex play.

Elsewhere I have argued that Shakespeare's dramatic form is a chiastic symmetry of three cycles of action: an initial two-act cycle, an intense one-act cycle in act 3, and a final two-act cycle.[24] Centering each cycle is an epiphanic encounter of remarkable intensity. At the midpoint of acts 1 and 2 is Lear's explosive encounter with Goneril (1.4.185–333). Her arrogant pride of power mirrors his own, showing the opposite of a godly ruler. This lesson is completed at the end of this two-act cycle, when Regan joins Goneril to humiliate Lear for his impotence.

A starkly contrary epiphany occurs at the midpoint of act 3 as Lear meets a naked, shivering demon-haunted beggar, an epiphany which mirrors Lear's new spiritual condition, bringing an incipient wisdom amid growing lunacy (3.4.24–183). That Poor Tom's obscene, disgusting wretchedness is being ***performed***, passionately ad-libbed by a former heir to an earldom who now humbles himself for survival, shows how epiphany takes on great complexity in Shakespeare's theater of wonder. A human being, an image of God, is forced to be a "poor player," and is himself transformed as his assumed madness mirrors a king's genuine lunacy—an astonishing rendering of epiphany!

The third and most moving epiphany occurs at the midpoint of acts 4 and 5 when Lear wakes from his madness to see Cordelia (4.7.12–90).[25] For many viewers this scene is the play's only genuine epiphany. But without the earlier ones—Goneril's godless smirk culminating in the devastating ensemble-shaming that ends acts 1 and 2, followed by the focus in act 3 on a wretched jittering screaming beggar, culminating in Gloucester's blinding—Lear could not fully "see" the epiphany of Cordelia. His vision of her absolute loving forgiveness does not, however, conclude the play. It is just the pivot in the final two-act cycle, which ends with Lear carrying or dragging in Cordelia's body and howling like a beast. This desolate scene in the play's initial quarto version is Shakespeare's most dreadful depiction of a "negative epiphany." It is his "black hole," paralyzing

---

[24] See note 1 above.

[25] Lear identifies Cordelia as "a soul in bliss," while he is "bound upon a wheel of fire / That mine own tears do scald like molten lead."

his genius to such a degree that Lear's primal howl quickly shrinks to snuffing out his grief in mute grunts of nothingness: "O, o, o, o."

Incurable optimists like me will quickly resort to the later, folio version of the play, in which Lear's final words invite us to a surprising vision: "Look there! Look there!" Their excited upward lilt urges us to conspire with the playwright by forming, each in his own way, a true reading of Shakespeare's most meaningful and carefully composed epiphany.[26]

Emory & Henry College

---

[26] For fuller commentary on *King Lear*'s folio ending, see the works cited in note 1 above.

Between the "triple pillar" and "mutual pair": Love, Friendship, and Social Networks in *Antony and Cleopatra*

Jonathon Shelley

I N act 4, scene 1 of William Shakespeare's *Julius Caesar*, Antony engages in what might best be described as a bit of social trimming. Having just successfully recruited the mass of plebeians with his inviting speech to "Friends, Romans, countrymen" and established his triumvirate with Octavius Caesar and Lepidus, Antony proceeds, somewhat antithetically, to determine who shall die and who shall live in the coming conflict. First is Lepidus's brother, who Lepidus agrees to have killed, followed by Publius, Antony's sister's son, who Lepidus points out "Upon condition . . . shall not live." Antony agrees, and "with a spot . . . damn[s] him" (4.1.1–5).[1] But when Lepidus exits, Antony goes so far as to question the makeup of his own triumvirate and Lepidus's own inclusion in the group. "This is a slight, unmeritable man," Antony posits; "Is it fit, / The threefold world divided, he should stand / One of the three to share it?" (3.3.12–14). An implicit hierarchy exists among the three members of the triumvirate, and Antony would rather it be the better duo—he and the younger Caesar—rather than a trio that comes to control the world.

Therefore, it is somewhat striking that *Antony and Cleopatra*, an effective sequel to the events of *Julius Caesar*, opens with a clear affirmation that the world remains a tripartite affair. "Take but good

---

[1] William Shakespeare, *Julius Caesar* in *The Norton Shakespeare*, ed. Stephen Greenblatt (New York: Norton, 2008). All references to *Julius Caesar* are to this edition.

note," Philo declares as Antony first enters, "and you shall see in him the triple pillar of the world" (1.1.11–13).[2] Despite Antony's most ardent of intentions, the third man remains, and the desire for the exclusiveness of the pair still seems to be running up against the larger collective of the trio. Antony has an exclusive conception of social organization that seeks to privilege the most exemplary of individuals, but such an ideal remains caught up in the reality of an existing set of commitments.

Antony's desire to cull his social circle from three to two may seem like the personal and perhaps even momentary whims of one man, but it reflects a prevalent social tension in the early modern period. Works such as Laurie Shannon's *Sovereign Amity* and Tom MacFaul's *Male Friendship in Shakespeare and his Contemporaries* have documented the ways in which the early modern period celebrated the classical tenets of likeness and parity in friendship which led to a valorization of exclusive, often identical social pairs; however, these critics have also shown how such celebrations of likeness proved unsustainable in the face of very real political and social differences.[3] Taking into account these social differences, more recent criticism has argued that the group, rather than the dyad, serves as the most potent paradigm for interpreting the social organization and development of the early modern period. As Hannah Chapelle

---

[2] William Shakespeare, *Antony and Cleopatra* in *The Norton Shakespeare*, ed. Stephen Greenblatt (New York: Norton, 2008). All references to *Antony and Cleopatra* are to this edition.

[3] As Shannon explains, the early modern idea that friends were "two sovereigns" or two self-actualized and self-determinant individuals offered a "sharp counterpoint to the terms understood to hold within the hierarchical relations of monarchical society." At the same time, the emphasis on friends as "sovereigns" served as a constant reminder that such dyadic equality was conceivable only in the specter of a monarchical political order. See Shannon, *Sovereign Amity: Figures of Friendship in Shakespearean Contexts* (Chicago: Univ. of Chicago Press, 2002), 7–9. MacFaul similarly acknowledges that the idea of the friend as a "second self" was a "persistent ideological force" thanks to the classical notions of Cicero and Aristotle; however, he argues that such "idealization" was also a "will o' the wisp" in the face of the inevitable differentiation that friends discovered between themselves. See MacFaul, *Male Friendship in Shakespeare and His Contemporaries* (London: Cambridge Univ. Press, 2007), 6–7 and 2.

Wojciehowski writes in *Group Identity in the Renaissance World*, "[t]he era that Burckhardt characterized as a rebirth is now being imagined through a different subtending metaphor: the network." Such a paradigm "encompasses a much larger geographic area (e.g., the world, or much of it), and locates the sources of transformation, however imagined, within an accelerating process of [synchronic] exchanges."[4] Likewise focusing on the increased prevalence of exchange in the period, John S. Garrison argues in *Friendship and Queer Theory in the Renaissance* that early modern writers "put pressure on the classical friendship ideal as a dyadic unit . . . composed of equals" and, on account of the period's expanding opportunities for economic and material gain, began to valorize friendship in groups.[5] To think of it more concretely in the context of *Julius Caesar* and *Antony and Cleopatra*, we might note that expanding military ambition calls for a literal group of participants but also a willingness to collaborate with less than exemplary figures, "unmeritable" men, or literal "unequals."

However, as the scenes from *Julius Caesar* and *Antony and Cleopatra* suggest, the adoption of such friendly groups in a global context was not necessarily an automatic or facile endeavor. It is certainly not the preferred organization for the likes of Antony, and its cultivation seems dependent upon a certain set of less-than-favorable compromises. This essay explores the interaction between such visions of social pairs and groups through an analysis of Shakespeare's *Antony and Cleopatra*. Focusing on the transcontinental nature of Shakespeare's play, I argue that direct, one-to-one dyadic relations were increasingly difficult to sustain. As a result, various intermediaries become essential to the maintenance of social bonds. The necessity of these third parties requires the play to rethink the singular dominance of specific individuals and pairs and recognize

---

[4] Hannah Chapelle Wojciehowski, *Group Identity in the Renaissance World* (Cambridge: Cambridge Univ. Press, 2011), 13.

[5] John S. Garrison, *Friendship and Queer Theory in the Renaissance: Gender and Sexuality in Early Modern England* (New York: Routledge, 2014), xiiv. As Garrison succinctly puts it, "there was much money to be made and new ways to make that money" in the early modern period; thus, as "marketplace activity expanded," persons were eager to welcome as many economically beneficial actors or "friends" as they could (xxii).

the ways in which social community is the product of a complex, overlapping set of interactions. But the play goes on to emphasize a stubborn inability of its most notable male protagonists to acknowledge the contributions of supposedly less notable individuals. This leads to both an elision and outright condemnation of such social plurality, but it also frames the networked vision of social life as an alternative to the masculine emphasis of pairs, as well as a just means to challenge forms of political despotism. Shakespeare's framing of the vacillation between pairs and larger trios in the context of classical Rome casts suspicion on the absolute ideal of friendly equality in pairs. In other words, the metaphor of the network may not necessarily be novel to the early modern period. However, the pair is an organizing conception of social life that proves so culturally embedded that it is necessary to go back to classical antiquity to uproot it.[6]

Indeed, as if to remind us that the question of social organization is no passing fancy, the beginning of *Antony and Cleopatra*

---

[6] In tracing both the dyadic and tripartite relations in Shakespeare's play, my argument juxtaposes both romantic and friendly bonds between characters in Shakespeare's play. While I do not want to conflate romantic love and friendship, I think such a comparison is apt and necessary precisely because the two relations are often in service of the same fundamental social paradigm. As Alan Bray has shown in *The Friend*, early modern male friendship very often used imagery of the "married couple" and the "binding forces of betrothal" (20 and 24). In this sense, both marriage and friendship serve the purpose of organizing persons in terms of exclusive paired union. But as Bray has also argued, it is essential that we think beyond this "private" capacity and consider the way in which friends were part of a "larger frame of reference that lay *outside* the good of the individuals for whom the friendship was made" (6). See Alan Bray, *The Friend* (Chicago: Chicago Univ. Press, 2003). My understanding of romantic relations and friendships as networks stems from this idea that social relationships, most notably pairs, can and should be analyzed for the kinds of effects they produce "outside" of their one-to-one bond. Antony and Cleopatra are a compelling example precisely because they are a romantic couple whose eroticism leads to larger political and military possibilities, possibilities that require the participation of additional thirds. Broadly speaking, the characters in *Antony and Cleopatra* are frequently exposed for ignoring the "larger frame" of their relationships despite the significant place those individuals may have.

recapitulates the very triple-double tension that appears near the end of *Julius Caesar*. Roughly thirty lines after Philo declares the world as still "triple pillar"-ed, Antony offers a fundamentally different imagination of his social existence through an effusive celebration of the pair. "Let Rome in Tiber melt and the wise arch / Of the ranged empire fall!" he declares,

> Here is my space.
> Kingdoms are clay; our dungy earth alike
> Feeds beast as man. The nobleness of life
> Is to do thus, when such a mutual pair
> And such a twain can do't, in which I bind,
> On pain of punishment, the world to weet
> We stand up peerless.
>
> (1.1.33–40)

In celebrating his union with Cleopatra, Antony may have departed from a desire for a twofold alliance within the triumvirate, but he remains committed to a more exclusive vision of the world, one in which "peerless" dyads like his and Cleopatra's might ultimately rule.

And yet, it is Cleopatra herself who is quick to try to disabuse Antony of such an idealized social vision. "Excellent falsehood!" she scolds. "Why did he marry Fulvia and not love her?" (1.1.40–41). Indeed, as much as Antony would like to imagine himself as merely "twain"-ed or "pair"-ed with one exclusive other, he is bound to a much larger set of networked commitments. Cleopatra's retort, then, is not merely a jealous correction but the diagnosis of a fundamental problem: As much as it may be attractive to organize or imagine the world into a system of "peerless" dyads, additional agents always disturb such a tidy vision of the world. The pair, we might say, is never a pair *per se* but a fiction made possible by the willful omission of existing social arrangements and complexities.

It is these existing complexities and the need to acknowledge the dispersed nature of one's connections that provides the initial drama for Shakespeare's play. When Antony learns of his wife Fulvia's death mere moments after declaring himself "peerless" with Cleopatra, he arguably gets what he wants: a clean break from a persistent third and an opportunity to organize his social life into the paired structure he had initially envisioned. And yet, this serendipitous paring down that realizes a dyadic possibility prompts Antony to reengage with the third party he had once ignored. "There's a great spirit gone! Thus did I desire it," Antony confesses upon hearing the news of Fulvia's death. "What our contempts doth often hurl from us, / We wish it ours again," or, as he later puts it, Fulvia "being gone" makes her seem "good" in ways that she had not when she was alive. Ironically, the minute that the third party is gone, Antony wants it back, or at least is willing to recognize its significance.

Antony's proposal to return to Rome is spawned by a surge of feeling for Fulvia that also calls for a geographic gap, or as he concludes in the scene, "I must from this enchanting queen break off" (1.2.121–27). Of course, Antony's stated need to "break off" from Cleopatra is an acknowledgment of the ways in which his "idleness" (1.2.129) in Alexandria has caused him to neglect his military and political duties. But I also want to read this declaration as a significant recognition of physical presence, the way in which social connections often require a kind of in-person, direct contact. Antony recapitulates this point when he claims that "The business [Fulvia] hath broached in the state / Cannot endure my absence" (1.2.169–70), a reference to Fulvia's revolt against Caesar that Antony feels he must go resolve in person. But Antony's friend Enobarbus points out the impossibility of such social resolution in an expansive, multinodal world, acknowledging that Rome may be in need of Antony's presence, but "the business you have broached here cannot be without you; especially that of Cleopatra's which wholly depends on your abode" (1.2.172–74). By going to Rome, Antony may solve some problems with Caesar, but he will also create or leave many more problems with Cleopatra and Alexandria.

The fundamental irony that seems to gird Shakespeare's play, then, is the way in which any attempt at direct contact—an event that gestures towards the resolution of social rifts and the simplification of social relations—does not simplify matters but expands the number of social actors. Such a phenomenon is most immediately observable when Antony leaves and it falls upon the attendant Alexas to rehearse the absent Antony's speech and motions for a lovelorn Cleopatra (1.5.42–50). In this sense, Alexas becomes yet another mediating wedge between the "twain" relationship of Antony and Cleopatra. But it is even when characters literally face each other that they prove incapable of fostering any direct relationship and require the mediating force of a third. When Antony and

Caesar finally reunite back in Rome, the two squabble over a history of perceived slights until Agrippa proposes that they establish a "perpetual amity" through Antony's marriage to Octavia, Caesar's sister. "By this marriage," Agrippa declares,

> All little jealousies, which now seem great,
> And all great fears, which now import their dangers,
> Would then be nothing. Truths would be tales,
> Where now half-tales be truths. Her love to both
> Would each to other, and all loves to both,
> Draw after her.
>
> (2.2.133–47)

Octavia is a literal and necessary conduit to the relationship between Antony and Caesar—a relationship that by virtue of Octavia's presence is not direct or dyadic at all but contingent on the presence of an intermediating force.[7] Furthermore, Octavia's entrance puts us back into the tripartite relational mess that Fulvia's death had, it seemed, resolved. By the end of the scene, Antony is no closer to realizing a mutually paired relationship with either Octavius Caesar or Cleopatra.

Cleopatra appears more attuned to the inevitability of such social complexity while also remaining eager for the familiarity of the duo. When news of Antony's reformed alliance with Caesar through Octavia is first delivered to Cleopatra, it is metered out via a careful set of proclamations that, at first, assures the queen of a reformed dyad before revealing the underlying social infrastructure that makes the very arrangement possible. "Madam he's well," the messenger begins, "And friends with Caesar . . . Caesar and he are greater friends than ever" (2.5.46–48). This much gives Cleopatra satisfaction, and we can observe the shadow of Antony's dyadic social vision from *Julius Caesar*. But as the messenger prepares to

---

[7] Gayle Rubin and Eve Sedgwick have noted how this "traffic in women" serves as a foundation of patriarchal heterosexuality. More specifically, Sedgwick describes this phenomenon in *Between Men* as "the use of women as exchangeable, perhaps symbolic, property for the primary purpose of cementing the bonds of men with men." See Eve Sedgwick, *Between Men: English Literature and Male Homosocial Desire* (New York: Columbia Univ. Press, 1985), 25–26.

qualify this with a "But yet, madam—" Cleopatra immediately cuts him off and launches into a predictive speech:

> I do not like "But yet," it does allay
> The good precedence: fie upon "But yet"!
> "But yet" is as a jailer to bring forth
> Some monstrous malefactor. Prithee, friend,
> Pour out the pack of matter to mine ear,
> The good and bad together: he's friends with Caesar,
> In state of health, thou says, and thou sayst, free.
> (2.5.50–56)

It is revealed that Antony is also "bound unto Octavia," but Cleopatra's meditation on "But yet" reflects the anxiety that attends an expanding social realm. She expresses comfort around the "good precedence" of the friendship between Antony and Caesar only; she dreads the reality of more networked commitments that such a relationship involves. What is repeatedly foiled, then, is the very thinking that allows for dreams of twofold worlds and "peerless" duos. Figures such as Caesar, once a preferred individual with whom to share the world, become opponents to be managed only by lesser "friends" like Agrippa. In this sense, figures such as Octavia or Agrippa, while not necessarily preferred, are nonetheless indispensable when it comes to the maintenance of a global network.

Indeed, Antony seems to forego his strong, "peerless" preferences and convert to a more networked appreciation by the play's midpoint. As Eros reports to Enobarbus, Caesar and Lepidus teamed up against Pompey. But after having done so, Caesar rejects Lepidus in brutal fashion. "Having made use of him in the wars 'gainst Pompey," Eros explains, Caesar

> presently denied him rivality, would not let him partake in the glory of the action; and not resting here, accuses him of letters he had formerly wrote to Pompey; upon his own appeal, seizes him; so the poor third is up till death enlarge his confine. (3.5.6–11)

Having used Lepidus only to cast him out, it is the young Caesar who takes Antony's idea from *Julius Caesar*—to use Lepidus like an "ass [that] bears gold" before "turn[ing] him off" (4.1.21–25)—and actually sees it through. Yet Antony at this point opposes this action and reportedly "frets" at the thought that "Lepidus of the triumvirate should be deposed" (3.6.27–28). This is not to say that Antony now likes Lepidus: he reportedly brands the man a "fool" and is enraged that Lepidus allowed one of his officers to kill Pompey (3.5.15–18). Rather, in opposing Lepidus's dismissal, Antony recognizes the way in which security and stability are, somewhat strangely, more readily available in a dispersed social network. The man who had once been considered a political and military pariah becomes an essential piece of fabric in the world.

But if this situation represents the acceptance of a new, if not necessary, communal reality, a tacit resistance to such liberal sociality still exists. When Cleopatra humors the idea of conceding to Caesar as a means to secure her and her country's fate, a bitter Antony cannot help but use her multipronged social history against her. "I found you as a morsel," he rages "cold upon / Dead Caesar's trencher; nay, you were a fragment / Of Gneius Pompey's, besides what hotter hours, / Unregistered in vulgar fame, you have / Luxuriously picked out" (3.13.116–20).[8] Antony's charge of intemperance is hardly surprising given the longstanding misogynist assumptions about female sociality.[9] But it also exposes the way in which an appreciation of networked social existence remains variable, here split along distinctly gendered lines. In describing Cleopatra as a perpetual "morsel" and "fragment," Antony practically rescinds the idea from act 1 that she is capable of the closeness that would make for a "peerless" "mutual pair." At the same time, Antony's flitting between Lepidus and Caesar from before becomes a sensible means

---

[8] This is not the last and only time Antony lashes out at Cleopatra. After his loss to Caesar's forces at sea, Antony brands Cleopatra as a "triple-turned whore" who has failed to remain faithful, militarily speaking, to Pompey, Julius Caesar, and now him (4.12.13).

[9] Such prejudice is classical and contemporary. As Cicero claims in *De amicitia*, it is "helpless women" who are "least endowed with firmness of character" and thus desperate for "defence and aid." Cicero, *De senectute, De amicitia, De divinatione*, trans. W. A. Falconer (Cambridge, MA: Harvard Univ. Press, 1923), 157. In his essay "Of Friendship & Factions," Sir William Cornwallis declares that "woman is loathsome and flexible," and thus her friendship does not require the necessary "labour" or "difficulty" that the "certaintest" of friendships have. Sir William Cornwallis, "Of Friendship & Factions," in *Essayes by Sir William Cornwallis, the Younger*, ed. Don Cameron Allen (Baltimore: Johns Hopkins Univ. Press, 1946), 23.

of self-preservation while such mutability in the hands of Cleopatra is nothing less than betrayal.

Even when Antony dies, his story cannot help but be imagined as one of unwavering allegiance to friendly dyadic parity. Caesar, as if forgetting all the bad blood between his sometimes ally and other times competitor, declares Antony his "brother" and "mate in empire,"

> Friend and companion in the front of war,
> The arm of mine own body, and the heart
> Where mine his thoughts did kindle—that our stars,
> Unreconciliable, should divide
> Our equalness to this.
>
> (5.1.42–48)

Little is remarkable about Caesar's eulogy. It dwells on the tropes of classical friendship, right down to the claim of equality between Caesar and Antony.[10] But it is creative in that it is a pure social fantasy, an immaculately cleaned up version of their social history that, as the play demonstrates, is fraught with conflict and reliant on enabling figures like Lepidus, Octavia, and Agrippa.

It is the rank and file that seem to best recognize and understand the social fictions, such as Caesar's, that abound. In a brief discussion about Lepidus's apparent lack of drinking prowess, it is two servants that more or less predict the content—or lack thereof—of Caesar's eulogy. Reflecting on Lepidus's less than esteemed reputation, the first servant notes that "this it is to have a name in great men's fellowship" before the second diagnoses the unfortunate position is be Lepidus in a world that is so wont to see pairs: "To be called into a huge sphere, and not to be seen to move in't, are the holes where eyes should be, which pitifully disaster the cheeks" (2.7.11–16). The servants are astutely aware of Lepidus and his presence in the triumvirate's quest for empire. He is, after all, the focus of the conversation. But they recognize that he is already destined for a life of perpetual invisibility, one that will ultimately remember a pair and forget the lesser third, no matter how instrumental he is at times.

---

[10] See Shannon, 38–46.

Upon news of Lepidus's dismissal, it is Enobarbus who best describes the appeal but also ultimate importance of the three-part group. With only Antony and Caesar left, the "world," he says, "has a pair of chaps, no more." But he cautions against the conflict that will inevitably arise: "And throw between them all the food thou hast, / They'll grind the one the other" (3.6.12–14). Once you have the pair, you're all the closer to a singular one, a prospect that leaves all others cast out. Thus, a world of "peerless" favorites—Antony and Octavius only—may be an attractive notion, a way to finally privilege those we care about most. But it is also a dangerous arrangement that threatens to reduce the world to a social cipher, a place in which only one person will matter above all others. This is the ultimate reality of *Antony and Cleopatra*. For all its demonstration of social groups' and networks' inescapability, a very un-networked circumstance emerges in the end: Octavius Caesar's ascendance as the first Roman emperor. The struggle to pursue and preserve friendly groups and networks then is not just to give oft-neglected persons their proper due. It also serves as a tool for the marginalized to challenge and thwart the dangerous and undue dominance of singular persons. The trick is to keep the network in sight when persons are wont to forget it.

Georgia Institute of Technology

"Beauty Changed to Ugly Whoredom": Analyzing the Mermaid Figure in *The Changeling*

Kendall Spillman

I<small>N</small> Thomas Middleton and William Rowley's *The Changeling*, the duplicitous nature of Beatrice-Joanna has led some scholars to question whether her character arc is either a continual regression or a constant. Henry E. Jacobs notes, "rather than changing, Beatrice-Joanna may simply be exposing progressively more elements of her consistent personality."[1] He continues to address the concepts of character and perspective in a broader context, asserting that "the paradox of coextensive change and constancy is equally applicable to life as it is to art."[2] Indeed, Beatrice-Joanna's self-conscious mutability from chaste daughter of an upper-class family to conniving lover of her father's servant, De Flores, reveals a search for autonomy in an ordered and restrictive society. Moreover, this

---

[1] Jacobs insists that a distinction exists between "intrinsic change," or character morphing, and "contextual change," or "shift in context" (651). To account for the "paradox in change and constancy," he offers three "distinct perspectives"; the other characters' awareness of change, the "transformed character['s]" awareness of change, and the audience's awareness of change (652). To Jacobs, while Beatrice-Joanna's character appears to be a constant, the other characters' shift in perspective toward her is due to contextual changes. For more, see Henry E. Jacobs, "The Constancy of Change: Character and Perspective in *The Changeling*," *Literature Criticism from 1400–1800*, ed. Thomas J. Schonberg and Lawrence J. Trudeau, vol. 100 (Farmington Hills, MI: Gale, 2004). Originally published in *Texas Studies in Literature and Language*, vol. 16, no. 4 (Winter 1975): 651–74.

[2] Ibid., 652.

search for autonomy reflects the inconsistent categorizing of women in early modern Europe. Constance Jordan addresses how a woman's socioeconomic and spatial restrictions in the "domestic and private" realm, apart from the "civic and public" realm, were "predicated on a woman's limited or defective humanity."[3] This subordinate classification according to sexual difference, as sixteenth-century Venetian writer Lodovico Dolce attests, was the very reason that the woman was primarily educated in "religion and moral virtue; her salvation ... closely tied to her willingness to behave as a natural inferior."[4] Both the church and the law deemed that women were more susceptible to moral fallibility and therefore regulated their behavior and conduct to ensure that they were chaste, virtuous, and subservient to male authority. The perception of Beatrice-Joanna as morally corrupt, therefore, is as much of a social construct as her performance in the play. This binary depiction of the woman as both deviant of and compliant to social convention captures the essence of the siren, or mermaid, a popular figure in Renaissance culture.[5] Tara E.

---

[3] Constance Jordan, "Renaissance Women and the Question of Class," in *Sexuality and Gender in Early Modern Europe*, ed. James Grantham Turner (New York: Cambridge Univ. Press, 1993), 90–106.

[4] Quoted in Jordan, "Renaissance Women and the Question of Class," 93.

[5] Guido Ruggiero states that while heterosexual relationships were seen as the "sexual ideal of society" sexual identity was delineated on the basis of male sexual maturity; although homoerotic activity as a subculture existed during the Italian Renaissance, young men were expected to "make the transition from passive adolescence to active adult male heterosexuality." As the era progressed, societal tolerance for sodomy drastically weakened, for it was considered an immoral and socially irresponsible act (24). Similar anxiety over male social bonds, sexual conduct, and marriage also existed in England, with female sexual transgressions equally condemned, according to Frances E. Dolan.

While this paper focuses exclusively on the relationship dynamic of heterosexual lovers from the play *The Changeling*, the mutability of sexual orientation and sexual identity during the Renaissance era is duly noted and worthy of further examination, especially upon considering the cross-dressing performance aspects of Elizabethan theater. For more on the Italian Renaissance and sexuality, see Guido Ruggiero, "Marriage, Love, Sex, and Renaissance Civic Morality" in *Sexuality and Gender in Early Modern*

Pederson posits that ". . . those elusive and captivating hybrids, dominated the cultural imagination in early modern England in complex and multifaceted ways as they brought women and animal together," and moreover, "the woman was frequently represented within and integral to sixteenth and seventeenth century English culture."[6] *The Changeling* does not provide any visual or textual description of a mermaid, but its subtext uniquely posits the mermaid as a metaphor for Beatrice-Joanna's transformation from guileless to conniving, from chaste to sensual. Her actions reveal a fluid identity that has self-transformed from, and poses as a challenge for, delineated behavior codes for class, gender, religion, and sexual relations. In his introduction to *The Changeling* Lars Engle asserts that the "powerful depiction of public and private selves suggests that the outwardly polite behavior of [the characters] may actually mask violent and insubordinate desires for change."[7] Likewise, the mermaid spans otherwise demarcated lines "between the sacred and the profane," as a symbol of vice and temptation in an era that witnessed growing resistance to established religion and monarchical government.[8] Although Pederson makes legitimate connections to several well-known plays of the English Renaissance, she overlooks *The Changeling* as a prime example of how the mermaid figure manifests itself, in this case, within Beatrice-Joanna's amoral, contrary nature. Beatrice-Joanna's independent sexual desire makes her resemble the mermaid figure in her subversive use of sex and sexual knowledge as tools to arrogate power, actions which represent a failure of the individual to conform to society and repent against sin, and which

---

Europe, ed. James Grantham Turner (Cambridge: Cambridge Univ. Press, 1993), 10–28. For further analysis of sexuality and gender in England, see Frances E. Dolan, "Gender and Sexuality in Early Modern England," in *Gender, Power, and Privilege in Early Modern Europe*, ed. Jessica Munns and Penny Richards (Harlow, UK: Pearson Education, 2003): 7–15.

[6] Tara E. Pederson, *Mermaids and the Production of Knowledge in Early Modern England* (Burlington, VT: Ashgate, 2015), 1.

[7] Lars Engle, "Introduction to the 'Changeling,'" in *English Renaissance Drama, A Norton Anthology*, ed. David Bevington et al. (New York: W. W. Norton & Company, 2002), 1594.

[8] Pederson, *Mermaids and the Production of Knowledge*, 24.

are therefore transgressions against the social and religious culture of the English Renaissance.

In *The Changeling*, Beatrice-Joanna's ambiguous nature stems from her willful resistance to her family's attempt to control her future. Her father betroths her to Alonzo, which Beatrice-Joanna laments because of her lack of choice in the matter. During a chance encounter with Alsemero, a prospective suitor who assures her of his honorable intentions, Beatrice-Joanna rejoices that she has met a man whom she finds physically and romantically attractive, claiming, "This was the man was meant me" (1.1.85). In other words, she wishes for Alsemero to replace Alonzo as her bridegroom in the conjugal bed; she seeks sexual fulfillment with a man of her choosing, not her father's. This attitude contradicts the socially prescribed marital role for women. Guido Ruggiero presents a reevaluation of Renaissance history, which "would center upon marriage, family, society, and the disciplining of the body."[9] He explains how the family served to empower the state by institutionalizing sex within an "ordered and disciplined Christian society," placing children in a "nurturing and moral environment" with an education centered on family honor and reputation, and reinforcing the social hierarchy by ensuring class-sanctioned marriage, which thereby ensured protection from "the dangers of love, passion, and sex."[10] While he acknowledges that the emphasis on sex within marriage is paramount for women due to the "honor dynamic that disciplined their lives and their sexuality," he also suggests that, "for Italy, and probably for other Renaissance cultures and societies, it is equally crucial to study the stresses put on this organization of marriage by what was seen as illicit sex."[11] Attempts to regulate sexuality were, among other things, a "desire to discipline and contain independent women beyond the family's control."[12] In an attempt to circumvent the role prescribed her and undermine the patriarchal authority, Beatrice-Joanna contrives to have her former fiancé murdered with the aid of her father's servant, De Flores. Then, in order to prevent her new husband from discovering her deflowering, she contrives to replace

---

[9] Ruggiero, "Marriage, Love, Sex, and Renaissance Civic Morality," 10.
[10] Ibid., 13.
[11] Ibid., 11.
[12] Ibid., 27.

her body with that of her maid. Ignoring the moral and social repercussions of pre-marital sex, murder plots, and family duplicity for young women, Beatrice-Joanna's singular focus on attaining knowledge in the carnal realm, as she tempts one man to marry her and another to seduce her, reflects the vanity and mutability of the mermaid figure. Just as the mermaid "fails to conform to one easily understood and interpreted role," instead serving a dual purpose in artistic renderings and textual depictions as tempter and seeker of knowledge, so too does Beatrice-Joanna defy expectations in her self-aggrandizing schemes and rejection of social mores.[13]

Sexual desire appears to be Beatrice's driving force, first for murder, then for marriage, then for protection. Readers may question whether Beatrice-Joanna's sexual repression overlaps with moral corruption, as an individual deprived of sexual pleasure before marriage finds a subversive means of fulfillment. As Pederson attests, "the mermaid therefore becomes a way to . . . picture the body, especially the sexed and gendered body that resists clear categorical frameworks and that holds erotic potential."[14] Although Beatrice-Joanna initially is reluctant, fearing the consequences of premarital sex, she still allows De Flores to seduce her (presumably) more than once. De Flores even marvels at "how the turtle pants!" as she responds favorably to his lovemaking (3.4.170). Beatrice-Joanna's initial revulsion to De Flores suggests that she feels unguarded and vulnerable in his presence, as she struggles with the bounds of social propriety, and cannot self-disguise before someone who possess the same deviant nature. Here, the aforementioned discussion of the class and gender restrictions in early modern Europe requires further emphasis. As Ruggiero mentions, society regarded love as a "dangerous emotion" unsuited for a marital alliance, yet premarital sex occurred on "all social levels" and both male and female partners used it to justify marriage.[15] However, the relationship dynamic between Beatrice-Joanna and De Flores reveals the dangerous culture of illicit sex as challenging both the social hierarchy and the civic morality of marriage. De Flores lusts after his master's daughter as forbidden fruit; she represents for him the portal to social

---

[13] Pederson, *Mermaids and the Production of Knowledge*, 2.
[14] Ibid.
[15] Ruggiero, "Marriage, Love, Sex, and Renaissance Civic Morality," 18.

mobility and economic gain. Despite knowing Beatrice-Joanna's reluctance to him, he is determined to have her, evidenced by his bawdy innuendos of "thrust[ing] my fingers/Into her sockets here" (1.1.242–43). Interestingly, De Flores also evokes the image of the siren (synonymous with mermaid), a hearkening to the gender fluidity of the trope in its seductive traits.[16] Moreover, his character also proves mutable, as he "shift[s] from servant to master" following his mercenary transaction of Alonzo's loss of life in exchange for Beatrice-Joanna's loss of innocence, thus replacing Alsemero with himself as gaining "all the rights and duties that a husband would normally command."[17] Despite knowing the cost of sacrificing her honor, Beatrice-Joanna succumbs to carnal temptation, a bodily transaction that ensues in an internal conflict over her physical and romantic allegiance, as well as the fear of others discovering that she is no longer a virgin.

According to the prevailing model of sexuality for early modern Europe, which Greco-Roman philosophy, Christian theology concerning divine will, and the monarchical hierarchy influenced, Beatrice-Joanna would have legitimate cause to fear pregnancy after her intimate encounter. The generally accepted view of sexual characteristics (which reveals a fundamental lack of understanding of human anatomy), was in the "one sex/one flesh" model that posited that both male and female genitalia needed to reach orgasm in order for the woman to conceive; therefore, a woman could get pregnant only if she had achieved sexual pleasure.[18] Beatrice-Joanna's

---

[16] Pederson, *Mermaids and the Production of Knowledge*, 2.

[17] Jacobs, "Constancy of Change."

[18] Ancient Roman physician Claudius Galenus was chiefly responsible for the one-sex/one-flesh model, which asserted that male and female sexual organs were analogous and therefore their sexual experience was the same; this model remained the paradigm of human sexual anatomy in Europe until the eighteenth century. Renaissance medical illustrations even depicted male and female bodies as anatomical inversions of each other. This analogy could serve to account for the mirrored personality traits of Beatrice-Joanna and DeFlores, as well as provide a foundation to the sexual nature of their relationship in *The Changeling*. For more on the one-sex model's cultural influence in early modern Europe, see Winfried Schleiner, "Early Modern Controversies about the One-Sex Model," *Renaissance Quarterly*, vol. 53, no. 1 (Spring 2000): 180–91. For more on

aforementioned ear, which leads her to search Alsemero's bedroom for knowledge that her bridegroom may possess, and that she can use to protect herself, subtly hints of her sexual enjoyment (as the play suggests).[19] Upon entering Alsemero's closet, Beatrice-Joanna discovers a manuscript entitled "The Book of Experiment, Called Secrets in Nature," which contains tests to determine female chastity and conception.[20] Hoping that there are no repercussions of her sexual encounter with De Flores, she inspects a pregnancy test that involves giving the female suspect "two spoonfuls of the white water" (4.1.31). Again, Beatrice-Joanna's agency and desire for knowledge reflect her subversive nature in a society that condoned female sexual pleasure only within marital boundaries. Her illicit deflowering stands in stark contrast with the sanctified, baptismal purity implied in "white water," conjuring images of innocence and young motherhood. The instructions to the virginity test that she procures list a sequence of invoked oral responses: laughter, yawning, and hiccupping:

> . . . Give the party you suspect the quantity of a spoonful of the water in the glass M, which upon her that is a maid, makes three several effects: 'twill make her incontinently gape, then fall into a sudden sneezing, last into a violent laughing, else dull, heavy, and lumpish. (4.3.45–49)

One oral behavior is noticeably absent: moaning, which suggests that it demarcates the borders of sexual experience. Additionally, the submersion of the liquid substance, a visceral trait associated with

---

Claudius Galenus's medical contributions, see *International Encyclopedia of Philosophy*, s.v. "Galen," by Michael Boylen, https://www.iep.utm.edu/galen/, accessed June 28, 2019.

[19] This article corresponds with Frances E. Dolan's argument that the play does not "depict rape by statutes" that adhere to seventeenth century Europe, and acknowledges that it also could be "participat[ing] in sexual coercion," but opts to narrow the focus on Beatrice-Joanna's autonomy in the context of female sexuality. See Frances E. Dolan, "Re-Reading Rape in *The Changeling*," *The Journal for Early Modern Cultural Studies*, vol. 11, no. 2 (Spring/Summer 2011): 4–29.

[20] David Bevington, the editor of *English Renaissance Drama, A Norton Anthology*, included a text note that the content described is actually located in another work of French writer Antonius Mizaldus (1520–78).

the mermaid figure, alludes to the subversive nature of women's sensuality and power.[21] The implications concerning women's fertility and lifespan—from conception to birth to mortality as metaphorically represented in the submersion of water—further illustrates Beatrice-Joanna's internal conflict and subversive nature as she struggles with sexual autonomy. Her preemptive knowledge of these tests protects her from suspicion when Alsemero, prompted by his friends, decides to test her fidelity and chastity. She resorts to tricking her maid, Diaphanta, into taking a virginity test to prove she is innocent before insisting that Diaphanta replace her on "her sweet voyage" with Alsemero (4.2.124). The *OED* defines voyage as travel by sea for exploration and discovery. Meanwhile, the metaphorical language of "sweet voyage" is a nautical idiom referring to a maiden becoming a woman through sexual congress. Beatrice-Joanna, having already taken her "maiden voyage" with De Flores, is aware that she cannot deceive her bridegroom into believing that she has never experienced the sweetness of sexual exploration and discovery.

Beatrice-Joanna realizes that the state will not legalize her wedding to Alsemero until they consummate their marriage; she is contractually bound to one man while sexually bound to another. In this moral and ethical state of limbo, Beatrice-Joanna must continue to obscure her true character and motives from the others, a mermaid state which synchronizes with Frances E. Dolan's suggestion that "perhaps early modern culture was afraid of secret transactions

---

[21] Philippa Berry's contextual analysis of the mermaid figure in Shakespearean drama further elucidates the trope's function in English Renaissance theatre. Berry claims that Queen Gertrude's implicit comparison of the drowned Ophelia to a mermaid in *Hamlet*: "like a creature native and imbued/Unto that element," is a salacious reference to prostitution, "which associated submersion in water with sexual activity" as well as "a siren-like song" (27). Moreover, the double meaning embedded in Ophelia's death in water connotes a "pagan subtext," whereupon the implied death by suicide also bears sexual meaning associated with the Greco-Roman goddess of love and beauty, as it "encompasses imagery of birth or conception" (28). Berry also notes that in Neoplatonic philosopher Porphyry of Tyre's *De anto nympharum*, Porphyry declares that the inhabiting of water by souls is "a delight, not death" (28). For more, see Philippa Berry, *Shakespeare's Feminine Endings: Defending Death in the Tragedies* (London: Routledge, 1999).

. . . between men and women . . . perhaps the threat was of intimacy and secrecy as much as anything else."[22] Indeed, the male characters with whom Beatrice-Joanna forges intimate relationships eventually feel as threatened by her as much as they do by their rival. De Flores wonders at Beatrice-Joanna's disloyalty toward her father regarding her breach of trust over her betrothal by pledging herself to another man. He muses, "She spreads and mounts then like arithmetic," suggesting that her guile may stem from a loose nature incapable of filial or marital fidelity" (2.2.61–62). Beatrice-Joanna's seductive behavior incurs De Flores's rationale that she would consent to illicit sex with him if she would betray and murder her own suitors at the risk to her family's reputation. Later, he proclaims Beatrice-Joanna to be "that broken rib of mankind," a reference to Eve, who, according to Christian narrative, was the first woman who took of the forbidden fruit and sinned against God (ignoring his own complicity, as well as Adam's).[23] Eventually, Beatrice-Joanna's duplicity is revealed to the others, including Alsemero, who rejects her: "Here's beauty changed/To ugly whoredom" (5.3.207–8). This uneasy tension with and condemnation of female sexuality again hearkens to the significance of gender, class, privilege, and traditional values. Pederson suggests, "it is important to consider the mermaid's association with the lost soul in need of redemption," as she resembles a "combination of human and fish that Christ and his followers . . . claim that they seek," and moreover, "a soul is achieved through either forced or voluntary marriage," which is a "prominent feature in British folk tales."[24] Beatrice-Joanna has two chances to prove her honor and loyalty both to her family and to the men to whom she is betrothed, one coerced, and the other voluntarily, but she fails each time due to succumbing to the sins of murder, debauchery, and intrigue. From the moral worldview of the church pulpit, Beatrice-Joanna risks losing her soul, thus failing to gain redemption, and possibly entrance to heaven; moreover, she fails in the moral responsibility expected of women during early modern Europe. According to Merry E. Wiesner, "women who showed too much independence, sexually

---

[22] Dolan, "Gender and Sexuality in Early Modern England," 12.

[23] *The Bible*, Authorized King James Version (Oxford: Oxford Univ. Press, 1998), Genesis 2:1–2:2.

[24] Pederson, *Mermaids and the Production of Knowledge*, 12.

or otherwise, are generally punished in popular literature," and only chaste virgins, or women who demonstrated fidelity to one man, were rewarded in the end.[25]

However, Wiesner also addresses the problematic nature of using early modern literature as a reference to understanding perceptions of female sexuality, as both male and female writers displayed internalized misogyny in their writings. She recommends researching "women who deviated from acceptable norms of behavior" and court records of sexual deviancy to determine what types of behavior that society sought to control.[26] Sara Eaton also alludes to the tendency to project expectations of femininity in her rhetorical analysis of courtly love in the play. Beatrice-Joanna's struggle is inherently a struggle against the moral dichotomy in which both her betrothed and paramour view her as a woman. Unable to conceive fluidity in a woman's nature, the two men serve as foils to idealized female sexuality and oppressive male possession, whereas Beatrice-Joanna ultimately succumbs to their perception of her: "a mirror reflecting male desires, as a vehicle for their pleasures."[27] The mirror, frequently associated with the mermaid figure, according to Pederson, appears to "represent a penchant for narcissistic vanity, deceptive self-presentation, and dangerous female sexuality."[28] In

---

[25] Merry E. Wiesner, *Women and Gender in Early Modern Europe* (New York: Cambridge Univ. Press, 2000), 59.

[26] Ibid., 60.

[27] Eaton, "Beatrice-Joanna and the Rhetoric of Love in the Changeling." *Theater Journal*, vol. 36, no. 3, *Renaissance Re-Visions* (October 1984): 378.

[28] Pederson, *Mermaids and the Production of Knowledge*, 12. Pederson also cites that in his text *Iconologia*, a seventeenth century manual to symbolism in emblems, Cesare Ripa interpreted the mirror as "the true symbol of falsity ... possessing no reality" (14). Interestingly, most of Ripa's pictorial descriptions of mirrors contain positive associations with scientific knowledge and self-awareness. However, in his explanation of Fig. 338, *Falsehood*, Ripa describes the "figure of a gay looking woman ... in the attitude of holding up a mask" while beside her lies "a syren [sic] looking into a mirror" as a "figure of deception" (95). The pejorative connotations implied within the combination of masked appearances, female deception, a hybrid being, and mirror objects provide a cultural framework on the iconography of the mermaid figure in Renaissance culture. For more

The Changeling, no physical manifestation of a mirror appears, just as no literal embodiment of a mermaid appears. However, just like the mermaid figure, the mirror functions as a metaphorical device, framing both how Beatrice-Joanna is perceived by others, and how she alters her image between public and private realms, reflecting in the end a distorted image, a changeling, shapeshifter, mermaid. In her essay "Visual Pleasure and Narrative Cinema," Laura Mulvey asserts that the male gaze constitutes an "active/passive split," whereupon women represent sexual objectifications of male desire to be "looked at and displayed."[29] As much as possible, Beatrice-Joanna attempts to assume the (male) gaze in an effort to subvert or redirect it from herself, whether it is toward another suitor at the play's inception, or attempting to manipulate her servants, male and female, to salvage her reputation.[30] By the play's end, she becomes compelled to face her own moral degradation: "Look no more upon't," she begs her cuckolded husband, unable to endure a witness to her public reveal (5.3.160). Woefully acknowledging that she could not accept what fate had in store for her, she reveals how deep her struggle to attain autonomy and how much she laments her failure: "my loathing/Was prophet to the rest, but n'er believed" (5.3.165–66). Regardless of her culpability in the play, she is inherently a product of sociocultural bias towards female sexuality.

Charleston Southern University

---

information on iconography, see Cesare Ripa, *Iconology, Or A Collection of Emblematical Figures Containing Four Hundred and Twenty-Four Remarkable Subjects, In Which Are Displayed the Beauty of Virtue and Deformity of Vice. The Figures Are Engraved by The Most Capital Artists, From Original Designs*, ed. George Richardson (London: G Scott, 1779), https://play.google.com/books/reader?id=fbKIOA_P8SEC&hl=en&pg=GBS.PP7.

[29] Laura Mulvey, "Visual Pleasure and Narrative Cinema," *Screen* vol. 16, no. 3 (Autumn 1975): 6–18. Reprint. *Contemporary Film Theory*, ed. Anthony Easthorpe (London: Longman Group, 1993): 111–24.

[30] Pederson also asserts that early modern culture posits the mermaid figure as dangerous "precisely because she has the potential to reconstitute those who gaze on her," going further to comment that this is why "antitheatrical texts cite the mermaid as a metaphor for theater itself" (69).

Imagining the Other in a Cuzco Defense of the Eucharist

Lisandra Estevez

THE Mint Museum in Charlotte, North Carolina possesses a fascinating late seventeenth- to early eighteenth-century painting by the Cuzco school of painting known as the Defense of the Sacrament or the Defense of the Eucharist as the subject is also known and will be subsequently referred to in this essay. The Mint's *Defense of the Eucharist* (fig. 1) represents the king of Spain, possibly Charles II (r. 1665–1700), and Muslims beholding the Eucharist, and is intended to promote the image of the Spanish monarch as a defender of the Catholic faith. A soldier sporting a feathered helmet protects the king. A lion and orb appear underfoot as symbols of the monarch's power. Brandishing his sword, the king defends the Eucharist, the blessed bread wafer, ensconced in a jeweled, gold monstrance, from three Turks who unsuccessfully try to topple the structure with a meager ribbon. Presiding over this event, two coats-of-arms, presumably the king's, flank an image of Christ as *Pantocrator*, or ruler of the universe, at the top and center of the composition.

An overlooked painting in the complicated history of viceregal Peruvian art, and a significant example of its kind, the Mint's *Defense of the Eucharist* makes a bold statement about the processes of evangelization and acculturation that unfolded with the Spanish colonization of the Andes.[1] In all likelihood painted by an Amerindian artist,

---

[1] The imagery of the Defense of the Eucharist follows the trajectory of the pre-Independence period (from the 1670s to late 1800s) in colonial Peru and Bolivia. For a systematic study of Peruvian imagery, see Annick Benavides, "The Cusco School Defense of the Eucharist: A Tribute to

Figure 1. *Defense of the Sacrament (Defense of the Eucharist)*, ca. 1750–1775.
Peru, late seventeenth to early eighteenth century, oil on cloth. Paul and
Virginia Gifford Collection. Museum Purchase: Mint Museum Auxiliary Fund.
1994.102.9. Collection of the Mint Museum, Charlotte, North Carolina.

this image envisions the complex relationships among art, politics, religion, and rhetoric in viceregal Peru. It visualizes the exer-
tion of European cultural control over non-European peoples and

---

Tinku" (MA thesis, University of New Mexico, 2014) and for Bolivian
examples, see Ramón Mujica Pinilla, "The Pillars of Hercules in Charcas:
Imperial Visual Politics in Viceregal Art in Bolivia," in *The Art of Painting in Colonial Bolivia*, ed. Suzanne L. Stratton-Pruitt (Philadelphia: St.
Joseph's Univ. Press, 2017), 83–138. To my knowledge, the only catalogue
that published the Mint Museum's painting is Charles L. Mo, *Splendors of
the New World: Spanish Colonial Works from the Viceroyalty of Peru* (Charlotte, NC: The Mint Museum of Art, 1992), 62.

underscores the power of the Iberian crown to maintain religious homogeneity. It poignantly draws parallels between Muslim communities on the continent, and, by extension, Amerindian societies in the Americas. The painting, I suggest, connotes the othering of *Morisco*, Spanish Muslims who converted to Christianity, and Amerindian populations under Iberian imperial rule across two continents.

The Defense of the Eucharist as a Proto-Orientalist Image

The Mint's *Defense of the Eucharist* is representative of a larger group of paintings that represent the monarch's piety and his defense of Catholicism against both heresy and idolatry.[2] Images of Muslims, namely in the guise of Turks, which circulated in early modern European prints, might have made their way to South America. European prints of both Turkish men and women adhered to proto-Orientalist conventions of representation.[3] Women were represented with full head coverings and men sporting turbans as evinced in an illustration of *Saracen Costumes and Arabic Alphabet*, which is a miniature from the *Peregrinatio in Terram Sanctam* by Bernhard von Breydenbach (1486, illustrations by Erhard Reuwich, Musée Carnavalet, Paris, France).

European travel writers often associated certain Islamic traditions with Peruvian Amerindian communities. José de Acosta's references to Muslims in the *Historia natural y moral de las*

---

[2] Francisco Montes González, "La herejia islamica en el imaginario americano," in *Arte a los confines del imperio. Visiones hispanicas de otros mundos*, ed. Inmaculada Rodríguez and Victor Mínguez (Castello: Universitat Jaume I, 2011), 128–50; Ramón Mujica Pinilla, "España eucaristica y sus reinos: el santisimo sacramento como culto y topico iconografico de la monarquia," in *Pintura de los Reinos: Identidades compartidas. Territorios del mundo hispanico. Siglos XVI–XVIII* (Mexico: Fomento Cultural Banamex, 2009), vol. 4, 1099–1167.

[3] Orientalizing imagery was also pervasive in early modern eastern and central Europe. See Adam Jasienski, "A Savage Magnificence: Ottomanizing Fashion and the Politics of Display in Early Modern East-Central Europe," *Muqarnas* 31 (2014): 173–206.

Indias (1590) illustrate how Europeans envisioned "other" peoples according to certain tropes. In many passages, Acosta compares Amerindian practices explicitly to those of Muslims and Moriscos. In relating the Andeans' ritual killing of animals, he writes that "the method of slaughtering any livestock, large or small, which the Indians used in accordance with their ancient ceremony, is the same one that the Muslims have, which they call *alquible*, which is to hold the animal above the right arm and turn its eyes toward the sun, saying different words, depending on the type of animal that is being slaughtered." The Andeans, Acosta recorded, "fasted from morning until the star appeared, and then they filled themselves and did the zahor in the manner of Muslims." As for ritual baths, Acosta recorded that "these baths were also used by [the Andeans] when they confessed with a ceremony that resembles closely the one that the Muslims use, which they call the *guadoi* and the Indians call *opacuna*."[4] In a similar turn, the late seventeenth-century French chronicler Amedeé François Frézier (1682–1773) noted that the women of Ciudad de Los Reyes lived in homes with Damascene tapestries and that they seated themselves "along the wall, legs crossed on a dais covered with a tapestry as in Turkey."[5]

Andean *Defenses of the Eucharist* always present the Turks as enemies of Christianity or, more specifically, Catholicism. The Spanish were quick to draw analogies between the Turks and the reconquest of Spain and the conquest of the Americas.[6] Amerindian peoples thus were visually and conceptually linked to the image of the Turk or the Saracen in the European mind. Art historian Carolyn Dean has noted, "that the conquest of the Americas was, at times, perceived by those who participated in it as an extension of the Reconquista, and that certain chroniclers frequently referred to the conquerors as Christians—not only echoing the centuries-old confrontation between Muslims and

---

[4] José de Acosta's *Historia natural y moral de las Indias* (1590), cited in Karoline P. Cook, *Forbidden Passages: Muslims and Moriscos in Colonial Spanish America* (Philadelphia: Univ. of Pennsylvania Press, 2016), 172–73.

[5] Ramón Mujica Pinilla, "Apuntes sobre moros y turcos en el imaginario andino virreinal," *Anuario de Historia de la Iglesia* 16 (2007): 171.

[6] Teresa Gisbert, *El paraíso de los pájaros parlantes. La imagen del otro en la cultura andina* (La Paz: Plural, 2001), 264–65.

Christians in Spain—but fitting their American experiences into Peninsular tropes."[7] Early chroniclers of the conquest identified Andean shrines as "mosques" (*mezquitas*), and Inka rituals were often compared to Turkish and North African cultural practices. Furthermore, historian Sabine MacCormack also rightly argued that "we are not merely dealing with patterns of perception which were carried over from the reconquest of Granada: for the method which the conquerors of Peru used to organize newly subjected territory and people stems from the same origin."[8]

Violent religious campaigns were simultaneously waged against Morisco communities in Spain and Amerindian communities in Peru. Starting in 1609 by edict of King Philip III and under the auspices of Archbishop Juan de Ribera in Valencia and extending through 1614, approximately three hundred thousand to four hundred thousand people were expelled from the city.[9] Beginning in 1610 and continuing intermittently until the eighteenth century, some violent campaigns were organized in Peru to eradicate not only heresy but also clandestine worship even among newly baptized individuals. Peruvian Baroque artists conflated the image of the Turk or Saracen with that of non-converted or non-baptized peoples. An image from Felipe Guaman Poma de Ayala's *Nueva Corónica y Buen Gobierno* (1615; fig. 2) represents two Inka nobles sporting masques and tunics that disguise them as Turks, dancing inside a church and performing proscribed rituals before the sacrament of the Eucharist. During Holy Week, ritual dances during which performers masquerade as Turks were performed until recently.[10]

---

[7] Carolyn Dean, *Inka Bodies and the Body of Christ: Corpus Christi in Colonial Cuzco* (Durham, NC: Duke Univ. Press, 1999), 14.

[8] Sabine MacCormack, "The Fall of the Andes: A Historiographical Dilemma," *History of European Ideas* 6, no. 4 (1985): 422–23.

[9] Benjamin Ehlers, *Between Christians and Moriscos: Juan de Ribera and Religious Reform in Valencia, 1568–1614* (Baltimore, MD: Johns Hopkins Univ. Press, 2006), 126–50.

[10] Gisbert, *El paraíso de los pájaros parlantes*, 264–65; Berta Ares Queija, "Moros y cristianos en el Corpus Christi colonial," in *Celebrando el cuerpo de Dios*, ed. Antoinette Molinié (Lima: Pontificia Universidad Católica del Perú Fondo Editorial, 1999), 175–90.

Figure 2. Felipe Guaman Poma de Ayala, *Nueva corónica y buen gobierno* (1615), Drawing 295. *The Sons of Native Lords Should Dance before the Holy Sacrament during Liturgical Feasts*. 783 [797]. Reproduced with permission of the Royal Library of Denmark, Copenhagen (GKS 2232 4º).

Envisioning Otherness in the Defense of the Eucharist

The Defense of the Eucharist imagery thus envisions perceptions of alterity or otherness in the Americas.[11] The subject position of Amerindian peoples, as mediated through visual representation, has been studied by both art historians and literary scholars. Both Tom Cummins and Carolyn Dean have reappraised the complex cultural

---

[11] There is an extensive literature on this topic that is beyond the scope of this essay. See Carolyn Dean and Dana Leibsohn, "Hybridity and Its Discontents: Considering Visual Culture in Colonial Spanish America." *Colonial Latin American Review* 12, no. 1 (2003): 5–35.

attitudes and thorny nomenclature that undergird the very notion of representation in Amerindian and early modern Latin American images.[12] Barbara Fuchs has posed important questions about the very nature of mimesis in New World representations of the other. She argues that images of "cultural sameness" and "authenticity" or cultural purity were constructed by the Spanish. These arguments can be extended to the analysis and interpretation of art in viceregal Peru; while colonial images generally replicate Europeanized sacred subject matter and visual conventions, these troubling resemblances merit deeper inspection.[13]

The Defense of the Eucharist as a Military Miracle

While identifying a single or definitive image for this imagery is reductive, the Defense of the Eucharist imagery can be understood in the context of "military miracles."[14] The rhetoric of militant imagery in the Americas heavily draws on well-established chivalric tropes and European iconography and ideas.[15] Specific images support a long-standing agenda of intolerance such as the gruesome

---

[12] Tom Cummins, "A Tale of Two Cities: Cuzco, Lima, and the Construction of Colonial Representation," in *Converging Cultures: Art and Identity in Spanish America*, ed. Diana Fane (New York: Harry N. Abrams, Inc., 1996), 157–70; Carolyn Dean, "The Renewal of Old World Images and the Creation of Colonial Peruvian Visual Culture," in *Converging Cultures: Art and Identity in Spanish America*, ed. Diana Fane (New York: Harry N. Abrams, Inc., 1996), 171–82; Carolyn Dean, "Reviewing Representation: The Subject-object in Pre-Hispanic and Colonial Inka Visual Culture," *Colonial Latin American Review* 23, no. 23 (2014): 298–319.

[13] Barbara Fuchs, *Mimesis and Empire: The New World, Islam, and European Identities* (Cambridge: Cambridge Univ. Press, 2001), 1–8.

[14] Amnon Nir, "The 'Military Miracles' in the 1536 Siege of Cuzco," in *Unlocking Doors to the Worlds of Guaman Poma and His Nueva corónica*, ed. Rolena Adorno and Ivan Boserup (Copenhagen: The Royal Library [Museum Tusculanum Press], 2015), 269–90.

[15] Hernán G. H. Taboada, *La sombra del Islam en la conquista de América* (Mexico: Universidad Nacional Autónoma, 2004); see also his article, "El Moro en las Indias," *Latinoamerica* 39 (2004): 115–32.

Figure 3. *Saint James the Moor Slayer,* ca. 1725–1750. Peru, 18th century, oil on canvas. Paul and Virginia Gifford Collection. Museum Purchase: Mint Museum Auxiliary Fund. 1994.103.2. Collection of the Mint Museum, Charlotte, North Carolina.

Figure 4. Unidentified workshop, Peru, Cuzco, *Santiago at the Battle of Clavijo*, 1653, oil on canvas. Courtesy of the Carl & Marilynn Thoma Art Foundation.

Santiago Matamoros (St. James the Moor Slayer; fig. 3). According to legend, the saint came to the aid of the Spanish king Ramiro I at a battle in the town of Clavijo in 844 CE, a scene illustrated in colonial Andean painting (fig. 4).[16] This Peninsular trope is transformed into the *Santiago Mata Indios* (St. James the Indian Slayer) in the culturally diverse viceroyalty of Peru.[17] This process of Europeans suppressing native communities is already well traced in seventeenth-century chronicles such as Felipe Guaman Poma de Ayala's *Nueva Corónica* (1615; fig. 5) and is reiterated in Peruvian vice-regal painting into the eighteenth century.

[16] Suzanne L. Stratton-Pruitt, "Santiago at the Battle of Clavijo," *The Virgin, Saints, and Angels: South American Paintings from the Thoma Collection* (Milan: Skira, 2006), 114–15.

[17] See Emilio Choy, *De Santiago Matamoros a Santiago Mataindios* (CIP, 1958).

Figure 5. Felipe Guaman Poma de Ayala, *Nueva corónica y buen gobierno* (1615), Drawing 163. *St. James the Great, Apostle of Christ, Intervenes in the War in Cuzco.* 404 [406]. Reproduced with permission of the Royal Library of Denmark, Copenhagen (GKS 2232 4°).

Spain's religious history complicates the "othering" of both Muslims and Moriscos by Spanish colonizers.[18] The Spanish saw themselves as the vicars of orthodoxy and sought to eradicate heresy; for example, they persecuted Protestants for their different beliefs. To that end, they linked Protestant, Muslim, and Amerindian cultures and labeled them as heretical. Many of these alleged heresies involved two significant cases of abuse: the purported defiling of the Eucharist wafer and the rejection of the process of transubstantiation. Transubstantiation in the Roman Catholic tradition

---

[18] Louis Cardaillac, *Morisques et chrétiens: un affrontement polémique (1492–1640)* (Paris: Klincksieck, 1977).

is based on the miracle that the bread and wine consecrated during the Mass are physical manifestations of Christ's body and blood as it was offered to his apostles. The sacrament of the Eucharist, however, was initially denied to Amerindians and even newly converted peoples were forbidden from participating in Corpus Christi festivals and consuming the Eucharist.[19]

Eventually, that restriction was overturned. The Eucharist was celebrated both in conventional and traditional European ways and also in newer and more innovative ways particular to the viceroyalty of Peru. Processions and celebrations dedicated to the Eucharist or the Corpus Christi were traditionally held on Holy Thursday during Holy Week. In Peru, elaborate processions celebrating the Sacrament increased during not only the seventeenth century but also the creation of extraordinary vessels to protect and display the Host or consecrated wafer during these very same ceremonies. Peruvian monstrances that were used to show the Host were elaborate silver creations that progressively became more ornate or baroque in design throughout the seventeenth century.[20]

---

[19] The decrees of the Third Council of Lima (1582–83) decreed that both Amerindian and Africans peoples not be allowed to receive Communion without a written license from their parish or confessor:

> Nemo vero Indorum aut Aethiopum ad communionem recipiatur nisi proprii parochi aut confessoris licentiam scripto sibi datam ostenderit. (Ninguno de los indios ni de los negros sea admitido en la communion si no presenta una licensia por escrito de su párroco o confessor.) [Caput 20: De communion in Paschate/ Capítulo 20: De la communion en Pascua]

The transcript of the Third Council of Lima was transcribed in Latin and translated into Spanish by Francesco Leonardo Lisi, *El tercer concilio limense y la aculturacion de los indigenas sudamericanos. Estudio crítico con edición, traducció y comentario de las actas del concilio provincial celebrado en Lima entre 1582 y 1583* (Salamanca: Universidad de Salamanca, 1990), 138–39. See also Dean, *Inka Bodies and the Body of Christ*, xv.

[20] See the following link for an image of mid-century Peruvian monstrance: https://www.metmuseum.org/art/collection/search/197090.

Archbishop Mollinedo as a Patron and
Promoter of the Visual Arts in Cuzco, 1673–99

Public processions organized by different confraternities paraded the sacred Host during Corpus Christi processions. These parades followed elaborate routes that led to the city's cathedral. The celebrations in Cuzco started Thursday after Trinity Sunday and lasted for four days. The spectacle of the Corpus Christi processions is visualized in a series of paintings commissioned during the tenure of Manuel de Mollinedo y Angulo (1640–99), the archbishop of Cuzco from 1673 to 1699. Mollinedo was a member of the priesthood in Toledo and was later an incumbent of the parish of La Almudena in Madrid as well as a member of the Council of Castile. Mollinedo had an affinity for painting; he was a prominent patron of the arts who assembled a remarkable art collection that contained works by significant artists working in Spain such as El Greco (1541–1614), Juan Carreño de Miranda (1614–84), and Eugenio Cajés (1575–1634), and also commissioned projects from major Peruvian Baroque artists such Diego Quispe Tito (1611–81). Mollinedo sponsored an extensive urban renewal of the city of Cuzco that rebuilt churches and buildings that had been destroyed by the earthquake of 1650.[21]

The iconography of the Defense of the Eucharist has its origins in the art of the viceroyalty of Peru that encompassed Peru and also Bolivia.[22] It may have been initially based on an engraving, such an illustration for a book, though a precise source is uncertain. Art historians José de Mesa and Teresa Gisbert have suggested that the image was inspired by the loyalty of the Cuzco archbishop Manuel de Mollinedo to the Spanish monarchy, whose rights to the possession of Peru he defended on behalf of the Spanish crown.[23] Lucila

---

[21] Wuffarden, "The Rise and Triumph of the Regional Schools, 1670–1750," 321–22; Johanna Hecht and Elena Phipps, "Celebrating the Eucharist," in *The Colonial Andes: Tapestries and Silverwork, 1530–1830*, ed., Elena Phipps, Johanna Hecht, and Cristina Esteras Martín (New Haven, CT: Yale Univ. Press, 2004), 305.

[22] Francisco Stastny, "Iconografia, pensamiento y sociedad en el Cuzco virreinal," *Cielo abierto*, vol. 7, no. 2 (1982): 40–55.

[23] José de Mesa and Teresa Gisbert, *Historia de la pintura cuzqueña* (Lima: Fundacion A. N. Wiese: Banco Wiese, 1982), 308.

Iglesias has recently studied the diverse representations of Muslims in texts of the viceregal era. Her research suggests that the Muslim threat was not a real or menacing presence but instead used to create a symbolic image of an "other" who was an enemy of Catholicism.[24]

The iconography of the Defense of the Eucharist emerged during what has been termed the "Inca Renaissance" that was, in part, inaugurated by elite ecclesiastical patrons such as Mollinedo.[25] As Luis Eduardo Wuffarden has aptly noted, "It can be claimed without exaggerations that no other prelate of viceregal Peru used art and images so systematically and effectively, not only as a means of enhancing the glory of religious worship but also as a political weapon to strengthen his authority, since he was in constant conflict with local civil authorities and the regular clergy."[26]

In addition to the visual sources that might have shaped the iconography of the Defense of the Eucharist, literary or textual references were just as relevant. Archbishop Mollinedo possessed a library of 696 volumes.[27] While not a book owned by Mollinedo, a possible source for the composition of the militant Defense of the

---

[24] Lucila Iglesias, "Moros en la costa (del pacífico). Imágines e ideas sobre el musulmán en el virreinato del Perú," *Diálogo Andino* 45 (2014): 5–15. See also Efraín Kristal, "Goths and Turks and the Representation of Pagans and Infidels in Garcilaso and Ercilla," in *Garcilaso de la Vega: An American Humanist. A Tribute to José Durand*, edited by José Anadón (Notre Dame, IN: Univ. of Notre Dame Press, 1998), 110–24.

[25] Horacio Villanueva Urteaga, "Los Mollinedo y el arte del Cuzco colonial," *BIRA* 16 (1989): 202–19; Luis Eduardo Wuffarden, "The Rise and Triumph of the Regional Schools, 1670–1750," in *Painting in Latin America 1550–1820*, ed. Luisa Elena Alcalá and Jonathan Brown (New Haven, CT: Yale Univ. Press, 2014). See also Pedro Guibovich Pérez and Luis Eduardo Wuffarden, *Sociedad y gobierno episcopal. Las visitas del Obispo Manuel de Mollinedo y Angulo 1674–1687* (Lima: Instituto Francés de Estudios Andinos, 2008).

[26] Wuffarden, "The Rise and Triumph of the Regional Schools, 1670–1750," 322.

[27] The inventory of Mollinedo's library is kept in the Archivo General de la Nación in Lima, Peru. The scholar Horacio Villanueva has studied Mollinedo's library and art collection. For a discussion of how private libraries were not only essential depositories for knowledge but also generated significant knowledge networks, see Teodoro Hampe, *Bibliotecas*

Eucharist imagery derives from the frontispiece of David Schuster's *Mahomets und Türcken Grewel*.[28] It illustrates the militant Islamophobic imagery that circulated in early modern Europe. The book's text, wrongly and pejoratively, attempts to demonstrate the flaws of Islam as a religion and to train "Christian warriors" in the war against the Turks. The illustration represents a Christian warrior wielding a sword against a turbaned Turk, who presumably is running away. At the top and center, Christ presides as a Pantocrator. I propose that this frontispiece might have shaped the overall concept and composition of the Defense of the Eucharist. This type of imagery circulated widely in Europe, particularly in Spain, Italy, England, France, and the Netherlands. Here the bilateral symmetry of the composition and near-equal scale of the figures suggests that these characters are on an equal or near-equal footing. The Christian soldier in the Defense of the Eucharist imagery is personified by the Spanish king, who is always positioned to the right of the divine versus the Muslim soldiers who are placed to the left. These directions carry symbolic meaning and associations as the king is set on the right hand of the divine and the Muslim on the sinister left.

Staging the Battle between Islam and Christianity in Corpus Christi Imagery

Images of the Corpus Christi also illustrate the battle between Moors and Christians as intercultural and interfaith displays of cultural dominance and conquest.[29] In the famous series representing the Corpus Christi procession from the Church of Santa Ana in

---

privadas en el mundo colonial. La difusión de libros e ideas en el virreinato del Perú (siglos XVI–XVII) (Frankfurt: Vervuert Iberoamericana), 1996.

[28] Maria Paz López-Peláez Casellas, "La representación de los musulmanes en la Europa del Barroco: la construcción de identidades," *Storia dell'arte* 139 (2014): 103–12; David Schuster, *Mahomets und Türcken Grewel* (Frankfurt: Bibliotheca Nationalis Hungariae, 1664).

[29] Dean, *Inka Bodies*. See also Berta Ares Queija, "*Moros y cristianos* en el Corpus Christi colonial," in *Celebrando el cuerpo de Dios*, ed. Antoinette Molinié (Lima: Fondo Editorial de la Pontificia Universidad Católica del Peru, 1999), 175–90.

Cuzco, there is a representation of an ephemeral altar with Charles II atop, brandishing his sword to defend a monstrance set upon a column from the attack of a Turk who is standing on the other side. The turbaned Saracen represents, by extension, all non-believers. The fact that Charles II's devotion to the Eucharist was first widely publicized in 1685 allows art historians to date the processional paintings to at least 1685. The images of the Defense of the Sacrament similarly can be dated to 1685 and after.

The Spanish King as a Defender of Catholicism

The Defense of the Eucharist, as a militaristic image sponsored by Archbishop Mollinedo, portrays the king of Spain as a guardian of the Catholic faith and as an orthodox, imperial ruler.[30] The Habsburgs kings were absent rulers of a vast empire, and thus their images served as alter egos for them.[31] Portraits of Charles II were created and presented in the context of legitimization of power in a conquered territory, to show him as a protector and propagator of the Catholic religion or, more accurately, to "personalize" the Spanish Crown in a remote land, as seen here in this idealized portrait of him that ommitted the actual physical deformities that afflicted him (fig. 6).[32]

---

[30] See Suzanne L. Stratton-Pruitt, "The King in Cuzco: Bishop Mollinedo's Portraits of Charles II," in *Art in Spain and the Hispanic World: Essays in Honor of Jonathan Brown*, ed. Sarah Schroth (London: Paul Holberton and Center for Spain in America, 2010), 304–22; Carolyn Dean, "War Games: Indigenous Militaristic Theater in Colonial Peru," in *Contested Visions in the Spanish Colonial World*, ed. Ilona Katzew (New Haven, CT: Yale Univ. Press, 2011), 133–50.

[31] Francesca Cantù, "Ideologia politica e simbolismo religioso: la Monarchia cattolica e la rappresentazione del potere nel Cuzco vicereale," in *I linguaggi del potere nell'età barocca. 1. Politica e religione*, ed. Francesca Cantù (Rome: Viella, 2009), 421–56.

[32] Suzanne L. Stratton-Pruitt, "Portrait of Carlos II as a Child," in *The Virgin, Saints, and Angels: South American Paintings from the Thoma Collection* (Milan: Skira, 2006), 204–7. The interpretation of the king's body is also informed by Ernst H. Kantorowicz, *The King's Two Bodies: A Study in Medieval Theology* (Princeton, NJ: Princeton Univ. Press, 1957, rep. 2016).

Figure 6. Unidentified workshop, Peru, Cuzco, *Portrait of Carlos II as a Child*, after 1667, oil on canvas. Courtesy of the Carl & Marilynn Thoma Art Foundation.

This propagandistic image of the Habsburg king as the defender of the Catholic faith has a long history.[33] Beginning with Count Rudolf in the fourteenth century, the Habsburg dynasty had claimed the Eucharist as a special devotion. The origins of the subject of the Defense of the Sacrament or Eucharist thus coincides with the rule of Charles II, the last of the Spanish Habsburg kings, as a means of propagating dynastic continuity because Charles II died without an heir apparent. While there are no images of Charles II's predecessors defending the Eucharist against Turks, there are prints that show Philip II, his great-grandfather, and Philip IV, his father, as guardian of the sacrament; both of these men engaged in military campaigns against both Protestants and the Turks.

The Habsburgs' exaltation of the sacrament of Eucharist is also recorded in sermons by Jose de Espinosa Medrano (nicknamed "*El lunarejo*"). Espinosa Medrano's words exalt the zeal and religious fervor of the Habsburgs; one can imagine the resonance of his speeches coupled with visual images that promoted the might of these kings who were only familiar to Peruvian audiences through these two media:

> "No niego yo que los demás Reyes Christianos tienen gran parte en este zelo, pero Filipono se contentava, con su fee, que Pavón Real todo ojos, todo vigilancias, atendia a su culto con el cetro, con la magnificencia, con la espada. (298)"

> ["I do not deny that other Christian kings have much this much zeal, but Philip was not pleased, with his faith, the Royal Eagle was all eyes, all surveillance. He attended his worship with the scepter, with magnificence, with the sword."]

> "Vivid, pues, vivid, vivid Filipo Augusto, Monarca Grande: Triunfad de la muerte, pues en la Eucaristía arbolais los trofeos de la Parca, y el sepulcro, triunfad que ya adornan el victorial carro de vuestras virtudes la Religion, pisando Coronas, la Fe conquistando mundos, el Gentilismo adorando vuestros Templos, la Heregia lamiendo vuestras plantas. Triunfad, que ya de los balcones de

---

[33] Victor Mínguez's study discusses the portrait of Charles II in the broader context of the Habsburgs' self-fashioning. See *La invencion de Carlos II: apotheosis simbólica de la Casa de Austria* (Madrid: Centro de Estudios Europa Hispánica, 2013).

la Celeste Roma, repiten a vozes, Filipo viva. Que podemos acá responder nosotros, sino que viva muy en hora Buena, vida de gracia, videa de gloria. (301)."

["Long live, then, long live, long live Philip Augustus, Great Monarch: triumphant over death, because in the Eucharist flourished trophies of the Grim Reaper, and the sepulcher, triumphant already adorned the victory carriage of your virtues of Religion, stepping crowns, Faith conquering worlds, Gentilism worshiping your temples, Heresy licking the soles of your feet. Triumphant, soaring to the balconies of Celestial Rome, voices repeating, long live Philip. Here we can respond ourselves, if not that he lives greatly, a life of grace, full of glory."][34]

The worship of the Eucharist by the king, as represented in both text and image, remained deeply ingrained in the political and religious propaganda of the Habsburg dynasty.[35] Spanish monumental altarpieces such as Claudio Coello's *Sagrada Forma* illustrate the Habsburg devotion to the Eucharist.[36] The story behind this painting begins on July 17, 1572, with Charles's great-grandfather Philip II. A village in the province of Holland was attacked by pirates, who made their way into the town church. One of the marauders took consecrated hosts from the altar and trampled on them. Miraculously, the legend indicates, one of the hosts began to bleed, and the heretic immediately converted to Catholicism. The miraculous wafer, known as the *Sagrada Forma*, was eventually given to Philip II of Spain in 1594, where it joined an extensive collection of relics at El Escorial. Charles II is pictured adoring the Sagrada Forma,

---

[34] These quotes from Medrano's sermons come from José Antonio Rodríguez Garrido, "La exaltación religiosa del monarca en el Cuzco colonial: Espinosa Medrano y la tradición del sermon fúnebre," in *La venida del reino. Religión, evangelización y cultura en América. Siglos XVI–XX*, ed. Gabriela Ramos (Cusco: Centro d Estudios Regionales Andinos "Bartolomé de las Casas," 1994); See also Stratton-Pruitt, "The King in Cuzco: Bishop Mollinedo's Portraits of Charles II," 312–13.

[35] Marie Tanner, *The Last Descendant of Aeneas: The Hapsburgs and the Mythic Image of the Emperor* (New Haven, CT: Yale Univ. Press, 1993), 207–22.

[36] See Edward Sullivan, "Politics and Propaganda in the *Sagrada Forma* by Claudio Coello," *Art Bulletin* 67, no. 2 (1985): 243–59.

held aloft in a magnificent monstrance, in a painting by Claudio Coello; it is *in situ* in the sacristy of the monastery of El Escorial near Madrid.[37] Charles II had a new altar created for the sacristy that would be suitably grand for the venerated relic, and he and his wife Mariana of Neuburg were present when it was transferred there during a lavish ceremony in 1684 when the monastery was illuminated with thirty-six thousand candles. The painting and the iconographic details of the altarpiece emphasize, through the symbol of this particular relic, the personal loyalty of King Charles II and his dedication to the Eucharist.

Charles II's program of orthodoxy and intolerance of non-Catholic beliefs is staged in a large-scale canvas by Francisco Rizi.[38] A large auto-da-fé took place in Madrid on 30 June 1680 in the Plaza Mayor, presided over by the young Charles II (r. 1665–1700) and his mother, Mariana of Austria, who are shown here beneath a canopy. Organized by the Inquisition, autos-da-fé were public ceremonies involving prisoners condemned for crimes against religion. Rizi's canvas is the most detailed depiction of one of these events.[39] In addition, the painting's neat and compartmentalized composition offers a compelling parallel to the profoundly hierarchical structure of the Spanish court and close overlap within it between political and religious power. The facture of this painting coincided with a time when Spain's economy was in crisis and during which the Crown was no longer able to finance its ongoing campaigns against the Ottoman Turks.

In turn, the Andean ecclesiastical authorities who promoted the Defense of the Eucharist, such as Mollinedo, were sending an effective warning to those who might not accept the truths of the faith and were are at the same time demanding loyalty to the Spanish Crown, the armed branch of Catholicism. The bilateral symmetry of these paintings has been understood as a principle of design that

---

[37] For an image of Coello's painting, see: https://www.wga.hu/frames-e.html?/html/c/coello/sagradaf.html.

[38] See the following link for an image of Rizi's canvas: https://www.museodelprado.es/en/the-collection/art-work/auto-da-fe-in-the-plaza-mayor-of-madrid/8d92af03-3183-473a-9997-d9cbf2557462.

[39] Jonathan Brown, *Painting in Spain 1500–1700* (New Haven, CT: Yale Univ. Press, 1998), 234.

underscores the monarch as a defender of the Eucharist and also as a protector of the Spanish empire. Álvaro Pascual Chenel has identified the different variants and types of this imagery.[40] To make it more compelling, the Defense of the Eucharist was sometimes "Peruvianized" by adding Santa Rosa de Lima—the first saint born in the Americas as a support for the monstrance, thus symbolizing the increasing dominance of Creole society within the Spanish empire.[41]

Amerindian Responses to European Imagery

Amerindian responses to European iconography and ideas are remarkably complex and demonstrated that they were not passive receptors of European imagery. The Defense of the Eucharist imagery illustrates how local artistic motifs and traditions fused with European imagery and style. This tendency is also represented by comparable imagery such as archangels, devotional paintings to holy persons and saints, and devotions to the Spanish monarchy. In all likelihood, these paintings were made by Amerindian artists whose names remain unknown to art historians. In his history of the Potosí region of present-day Bolivia, Bartolomé Arzans commented on the industry and ingenuity of Andean artistry:

> "los de este peruano reino son de muy rara habilidad, pues se experimenta (con gran sentimiento de los españoles) el que los Indios se hayen alzado con el ejercicio de todos los oficios, no solo mecánicos mas también los del arte."

---

[40] Álvaro Pascual Chenel, "Fiesta sacra y poder politico: la iconografí de los Austrias como defensores de la Eucaristía y la Inmaculada en Hispanoamérica," *Hipogrifo* 1, no. 1 (2013): 57–86.

[41] Ramón Mujica Pinilla, *Rosa limensis: Mística, politica e iconografía en torno a la patrona de América* (Lima: IFEA, Fondo de Cultura Ecónomica, Banco Central de Reserva, 2001); Luis Eduardo Wuffarden, "Ethnicity, Religiosity, and Iconographic Innovation in Painting under the Viceroyalty," in *Peru: Kingdoms of the Sun and the Moon*, ed. Victor Pimentel (Montreal: Montreal Museum of Fine Arts, 2012).

["these [people] of this Peruvian kingdom are of exceptional ability because they experiment (with the great sentiment of the Spaniards) that the Indians have risen up with the exercise of all the trades, not only mechanics but also those of art."][42]

Moreover, the Defense of the Eucharist paintings demonstrate how Amerindians subtly subverted the conventions of European imagery thus complicating viewers' understanding of their subject-positions.[43] The bilateral symmetry of the Defense of the Eucharist imagery refers to Andean spatial hierarchies that manifested in the design and function of ceremonial objects such as kero cups.[44] The near-equal size and footing of the Turks, when compared to that of the king himself, indicates the Andean artists who painted these images saw the Turks not as defeated enemies but enemies formidable enough to confront and challenge the king.

The popularity of images such as the Defense of the Eucharist or Santiago Mata-Indios in vice-regal Peru might be challenging to grasp at first glance. Santiago's popularity among Amerindian populations, and especially the Andean peoples whose ancestors are trampled by the saint in some of these images, may seem especially difficult to understand. Cuzco school artists routinely represented these images. Even if asked to paint on commission, how could native peoples celebrate a hero of their defeat, the same figure whom Spaniards invoked to represent their military and social superiority

---

[42] Bartolomé Arzáns de Orsuá y Vela, *Historia de la Villa Imperial de Potosí* (Providence, RI: Brown Univ. Press, 1965), 20. See also Ricardo Kusunoki, "Esplendor y ocaso de los maestros cuzqueños (1700–1850)," in *Arte Colonial*, ed. Ricardo Kusonoki and Luis Eduardo Wuffarden (Lima: Asociación Museum de Arte Lima, 2016), 39–58.

[43] Carolyn Dean, "The Renewal of Old World Images and the Creation of Colonial Peruvian Visual Culture," in *Converging Cultures: Art & Identity in Spanish America*, edited by Diana Fane (New York: Harry N. Abrams, Inc., 1996), 171: "Although Europeans required at least nominal conversion for any natives wishing to participate in the colonial political, social, and economic order, native Andeans were not passive receptacles of Christian precepts, but an active, creative force."

[44] Tom Cummins, *Toasts with the Incas: Andean Abstraction and Colonial Images on Quero Vessels* (Ann Arbor: Univ. of Michigan Press, 2002); See also Benavides, "The Cusco School Defense of the Eucharist: A Tribute to Tinku," xiv.

in the Americas? Devotion to Santiago in the Americas, however, has been described as not only reinforcing Spanish hegemony but also simultaneously offering opportunities for resistance. At the very least the images have multiple meanings depending upon the audience. Scholars believe Andean Amerindians identified Santiago with lightning, one of the natural elements worshipped in local religions before the Spaniards' arrival. In the Andean region, missionaries facilitated conversion by drawing parallels between Santiago and Illapa, the god of thunder and lightning, even calling the apostle Son of Thunder. Native Andeans persisted in the celebration of the cult of Illapa through the Christian feast of Santiago well into the eighteenth century. Hence the miraculous appearance in the paintings confirmed the continuity of traditional beliefs under the new Spanish order. It likewise preserved the city of Cuzco as a vital ritual site for Amerindian audiences.[45]

The pictorial language of the Defense of the Eucharist thus illustrates an overlapping discourse of alterity and otherness in colonial Andean art. Among these many converging conversations, another point of comparison for Indianist discourse is found in the writings on Morisco culture. This conjunction is appropriate because official policy toward both groups followed a similar path until the beginning of the seventeenth century when the Moriscos were expelled from Spain. There were systematic attempts at conversion of the Moriscos, and the elaboration of policy concerning one group often took as its model a discipline that was applied to the other. The discourses through which these strategies were elaborated were remarkably alike, and so were the native Morisco and Amerindian protests against them. Both Moriscos and Amerindians were accused of apostasy and heresy respectively—even after submitting to public conversion to Christianity.[46] A closer examination of the Defense of the Eucharist within a literary context reveals

---

[45] Kelly Donahue-Wallace, *Art and Architecture of Viceregal Latin America, 1521–1821* (Albuquerque: Univ. of New Mexico Press, 2009), 157. See also Gustavo Navarro Castro, "Latin American Iconography of Saint James the Killer of Moors," in *America: Bride of the Sun. 500 Years Latin and the Low Countries* (Antwerp: Royal Museum of Fine Arts, 1992).

[46] Rolena Adorno, "The Depiction of Self and Other in Colonial Peru," *Art Journal* 49, no. 2 (1990): 110–18.

the complicated subject position of Amerindians. Did the Andean artists who painted this imagery necessarily identify themselves with the Turks as peoples whose cultures, beliefs, and traditions were "othered" by European colonizers?

Guaman Poma's *Nueva corónica* is deliberate in identifying the origins of Andean peoples and making a case for their humanity, which had been stripped away by European racial discourses. Guaman Poma claims that ancient Andean peoples were the original descendants of Adam and Eve, appropriating these first humans of the Bible as the "progenitors of the Andean race." In claiming the origins of Andean peoples, he staunchly states that Amerindians are Jews, contradicting a theory about Amerindians as one of the lost tribes of Israel. He also remarks that Amerindians are not Muslims or Turks and ultimately denies the non-Christian origins of Andean people; moreover, he makes the case that the ancient peoples of the Andes were highly civilized.[47] Furthermore, the Bull of the Holy Crusade *(Bula de la Santa Cruzada)*, first granted in 1089 by Pope Urban II, offered indulgences that permitted an exit from purgatory more quickly in recognition of service in the war against Muslims during the Reconquista. Tom Cummins has shown that these indulgences were prized objects, as some Andeans were buried with their copies of this document. These individuals purchased these indulgences to contribute to the church's campaigns against Islam, with the ultimate goal of gaining salvation.[48]

---

[47] Felipe Guaman Poma de Ayala, *El primer nueva corónica y buen gobierno* (1615), ed. John V. Murra and Rolena Adorno, Quechua translations by Jorge Urioste (Madrid: Historia-16, 1987), 60. In addition to her translations, Rolena Adorno has written extensively on Guaman Poma's chronicle. See also Rolena Adorno, "La Ciudad letrada y los discursos coloniales," *Hispamérica* 48 (1987): 3–24, and "The Depiction of Self and Other in Colonial Peru," *Art Journal*, vol. 49, no. 2 (Summer 1990): 110–18.

[48] Thomas B. F. Cummins, "The Indulgent Image: Prints in the New World," in *Contested Visions in the Spanish Colonial World*, ed. Ilona Katzew (New Haven, CT: Yale Univ. Press, 2011), 223–25. See also Cook, *Forbidden Passages*, 169.

The Defense of the Eucharist as a Transgressive Image

What do art historians then make of colonial iconography or images such as the Defense of the Eucharist? Ramón Mujica Pinilla has used the term transgressive (*transgredido/a*) to illustrate the process of religious syncretism and acculturation in colonial Andean art. This approach has opened up viceregal art to multiple cultural readings that privilege not only the agency of the colonizer but also the voices of the other or the oppressed. Ananda Cohen-Aponte has made a comparable argument about how the notions of temporality and symmetry in the colonial Andean world were deeply affected by racialized constructs.[49] The design principle of balance in Andean imagery can, thus, be understood in diverse and dynamic ways, in particular, in the Defense of the Eucharist iconography. For example, Annick Benavides has interpreted the symmetry in these paintings as an expression of Andean belief systems, namely the Quechua concept of *tinku*, which refers to the union of distinct or complementary forces to generate a new form.[50] Benavides notes that "[t]he immense popularity of the *Defense of the Eucharist* iconography can be attributed to a local Andean affinity for understanding triumph as the coming together of festive, complementary opponents."[51]

Artists continued to represent this struggle between European and Amerindian communities vis-à-vis the perennial struggle of Christianity. Through the eighteenth century, the Bourbon kings of Spain such as Philip V (r. 1700–1746) continued this iconography

---

[49] Ananda Cohen-Aponte, "Decolonizing the Global Renaissance: A View from the Andes," in *The Globalization of Renaissance Art: A Critical Review*, ed. Daniel Savoy (Leiden: Brill, 2017), 69–70.

[50] Annick Benavides, "The Cusco School Defense of the Eucharist: A Tribute to Tinku" (MA thesis, University of New Mexico), 9–10; Diego Porras Barrenechea, Raúl González Holguín, *Vocabulario De La Lengua General De Todo El Perú Llamada Lengua Qquichua O Del Inca*, Nueva, con un prólogo de Raúl Porras Barrenechea. Edición del Instituto de Historia. Ed., Universidad Nacional Mayor De San Marcos: Pub. Del Cuarto Centenario (Lima: Impr. Santa Marìa, 1952).

[51] Benavides, "The Cusco School Defense of the Eucharist: A Tribute to Tinku," 9.

Figure 7. Unidentified workshop, Peru, Cuzco, *Defense of the Eucharist by Philip V of Spain*, ca. 1700–1746, oil on canvas. Courtesy of the Carl & Marilynn Thoma Art Foundation.

(fig. 7).[52] Many similar representations were also produced during the reign of Charles IV who died in 1819, only a few years before many Latin American countries gained their independence. Given the wars of succession that transpired in Spain that challenged the legitimacy of the monarchy, the Defense of the Eucharist imagery continued to confer—without question—authority to absent kings who ruled by the virtual proxy of their swords.

Winston-Salem State University

---

[52] Suzanne L. Stratton-Pruitt, "Defense of the Eucharist by Philip V of Spain," *The Virgin, Saints, and Angels: South American Paintings from the Thoma Collection* (Milan: Skira, 2006), 132–33.

A Critique of Poor Reading:
Antissia's Madness in *The Countess*
of Montgomery's Urania

Rachel M. De Smith Roberts

Introduction

WHEN Mary Wroth published *The Countess of Montgom-ery's Urania* in 1621, she contributed to a long-running debate about the value and dangers of reading.[1] Reading in general was often thought to be perilous, and the popular romance genre was widely viewed as dangerous for early modern readers.[2]

---

[1] Mary Wroth, *The First Part of the Countess of Montgomery's Urania*, ed. Josephine A. Roberts (Binghamton, NY: MRTS, 1995). Hereafter cited as *Urania* 1.

[2] Wroth's particular approach to the romance genre is one of the most frequently studied aspects of her work, particularly as her writing re-envisions romance from a female perspective. I have found the following studies on Wroth's relationship to the romance particularly helpful: Heather L. Weidemann, "Theatricality and Female Identity in Mary Wroth's *Urania*," in *Reading Mary Wroth: Representing Alternatives in Early Modern England*, ed. Naomi J. Miller and Gary Waller (Knoxville: Univ. of Tennessee Press, 1991), 191–209; Gwynne Aylesworth Kennedy, "Feminine Subjectivity in the Renaissance: The Writings of Elizabeth Cary, Lady Falkland, and Lady Mary Wroth" (PhD diss., University of Pennsylvania, 1989); and Naomi J. Miller, *Changing the Subject: Mary Wroth and Figurations of Gender in Early Modern England* (Lexington: Univ. Press of Kentucky, 1996). See also Sheila T. Cavanagh, "Romancing the Epic: Lady Mary Wroth's *Urania* and Literary Traditions," in *Approaches to the Anglo and American Female Epic, 1621–1982*, ed. Bernard Schweizer (Aldershot: Ashgate, 2006), 19–36; Jennifer Lee Carrell, "A Pack of Lies in a Looking Glass:

As Tina Krontiris notes, "Moralists and theoreticians on education almost unanimously castigated romantic literature . . . especially for women."[3] In fact, in the wake of *Urania*'s publication, Wroth was reprimanded by one of her readers, Sir Edward Denny.[4] Denny chastised Wroth in a series of letters, accusing her of corrupting her readers with "lascivious tales and amorous toyes" (239).[5] Given both

---

Lady Mary Wroth's *Urania* and the Magic Mirror of Romance," *Studies in English Literature, 1500–1900*, 34, no. 1 (1994): 79–107; Helen Hackett, "'Yet tell me some such fiction': Lady Mary Wroth's *Urania* and the 'Femininity' of Romance," in *Women, Texts and Histories 1575–1760*, ed. Clare Brant and Diane Purkiss (London: Routledge, 1992), 39–68; and Cynthia Marie Baer, "Wise and Worthier Women: Lady Mary Wroth's 'Urania' and the Development of Women's Narrative" (PhD diss., University of Washington, 1993).

[3] Tina Krontiris, "Breaking Barriers of Genre and Gender: Margaret Tyler's Translation of *The Mirrour of Knighthood*," *English Literary Renaissance* 18, no. 1 (1988): 19–39; here 23–24. The classic studies on early modern women's reading and writing remain Ruth Kelso's *Doctrine for the Lady of the Renaissance* (Urbana: Univ. of Illinois Press, 1978) and Elaine Beilin's *Redeeming Eve* (Princeton, NJ: Princeton Univ. Press, 1987), although more recent studies, such as Laura Lunger Knoppers's introduction to *The Cambridge Companion to Early Modern Women's Writing* (Cambridge: Cambridge Univ. Press, 2009), push back against the narrative of the suppressed woman reader and writer.

[4] Josephine Roberts reproduces Denny's poem and Wroth's reply in the introduction to *The Poems of Lady Mary Wroth* (Baton Rouge: Louisiana State Univ. Press, 1983), 32–33, 34–35. Denny and Wroth also exchanged several letters on the subject, which are included in Roberts as an appendix, 233–46. All quotations from these poems and letters in this essay are taken from Roberts's text.

[5] Sir Edward Denny apparently (and probably correctly) interpreted an episode in *Urania* 1, in which Sirelius must defend his unfaithful wife against her father's violence, as being inspired by his daughter Honoria's unhappy marriage to James Hay (c. 1580–1636), later first earl of Carlisle (Wroth, *The First Part*, 778n515.9). His ire took the form of a scathing poetic critique, entitled "To Pamphilia from the father-in-law of Sirelius," in which he castigates Wroth as a "monster" (line 1). The title suggests that Denny, unsurprisingly, took particular offense at Wroth's description of the said father-in-law as "a phantastical thing, vaine as Courtiers, rash as madmen, and ignorant as women" *Urania* 1:516.7–8.

the early modern suspicion of reading and Denny's response, it is not surprising that Wroth also addresses the dangers of reading in her manuscript sequel to *Urania*.[6] Of particular interest is an episode in which a woman named Antissia goes mad from reading too much. On its surface, this episode supports common early modern concerns about reading—and women. Antissia's madness is caused by reading and is described by other characters as a particularly feminine affliction. Furthermore, her madness manifests in the creation of poetry that other characters condemn in terms strikingly similar to those Denny used for Wroth's work. However, as I argue, beneath the surface of this episode lies a pointed critique of the belief that reading is dangerous. All of Antissia's problems arise, ultimately, not from her own choice to read certain things but from the bad reading and interpretation practiced by other characters.

Wroth's critique of poor reading in this episode draws on the literary ancestor of the reading-mad Antissia: Don Quixote.[7] As Josephine Roberts argues, Cervantes's *Don Quixote*, particularly Thomas Shelton's English translation (1612/1620), signifi-

---

[6] Mary Wroth, *The Second Part of The Countess of Montgomery's Urania*, ed. Josephine A. Roberts, Suzanne Gossett, and Janel Mueller (Tempe, AZ: ACMRS, 1999), hereafter cited as *Urania* 2. Studies exclusively about the *Urania* sequel are rare; one example is Clare R. Kinney, "'Beleeve this butt a fiction': Female Authorship, Narrative Undoing, and the Limits of Romance in *The Second Part of the Countess of Montgomery's Urania*," *Spenser Studies* 17 (2003): 239–50.

[7] Miguel de Cervantes, *Don Quixote*, trans. P. A. Motteux (New York: Knopf, 1991). All quotations are from this edition, given in text as Cervantes followed by the page number. Distilling the scholarly discussion about *Don Quixote* is an impossible (not to say maddening) task; for this paper I consulted A. J. Close's introduction to the Motteux translation cited above as well as the following articles, both of which have extensive introductory sections detailing scholarly approaches: Milan Vidaković, "Irony Called into Question: *Don Quixote*'s Alazon and Eiron," *Papers on Language and Literature* 53, no. 2 (Spring 2017): 166–90; Jed Rasula, "When the Exception Is the Rule: *Don Quixote* as Incitement to Literature," *Comparative Literature* 51, no. 2 (Spring 1999): 123–51. I also found Dale Shuger's *Don Quixote in the Archives: Madness and Literature in Early Modern Spain* (Edinburgh: Edinburgh Univ. Press, 2012) to be invaluable for historical context.

cantly influenced Wroth.[8] *Don Quixote* does not form the basis for many episodes in *Urania*. However, Roberts notes that Cervantes's romance "guided [Wroth's] response to a range of her more direct sources."[9] In other words, Cervantes's satirical perspective toward the romance genre influences Wroth's overall attitude in her work. This influence is often seen in the ironic tone that Wroth's narrator takes toward events in the tale. For instance, this narrative comment from *Urania* 1: "It being impossible for Knights and Ladies to travel without adventures, this befell them" (*Urania* 1:397.40–41). Roberts notes that "adventures" is the term Shelton uses in his translation of *Don Quixote* "to highlight the basically self-centered nature of most chivalric activity."[10] Wroth's chosen term thus directly evokes *Don Quixote* even as she comments on the romance genre as a whole.

As she does with most source material, however, Wroth uses the basic structure of *Don Quixote* for her own purposes—in this case, warning her readers about the dangers of poor interpretation. This essay examines the episode of Antissia's madness, paying particular attention to the causes of her madness as well as to the manifestation of her madness through poetry. I will offer some brief comparisons with *Don Quixote*, the inspiration for this episode; I will also note some moments where Denny's real-life critique of Wroth aligns with Antissia's experience. By incorporating material from both Cervantes and Denny, my reading of this episode reinforces Wroth's general goal in *Urania* to reframe reading and the romance around women's experiences. All of these comparisons, both literary and historical, contribute to Wroth's use of this episode as a condemnation of poor reading. Wroth ultimately posits that reading certain things is not, as many of her contemporaries believed, dangerous. Rather, being a poor reader causes harm. In this episode, the one being harmed is Antissia, whose poetry (like Wroth's) is condemned by the poor readers around her.

---

[8] Wroth, *The First Part*, xx. See also Carrell, "A Pack of Lies," 100.

[9] Wroth, *The First Part*, xx.

[10] Wroth, *The First Part*, xxiii.

Antissia's Madness: Reading in Bad Company

To begin at the beginning: The concept of literary madness clearly draws inspiration from *Don Quixote*:

> [He] gave himself up so wholly to the reading of Romances, that a-Nights he would pore on 'till 'twas day, and a-Days he would read on 'till 'twas Night; and thus by sleeping little, and reading much, the Moisture of his Brain was exhausted to that Degree, that at last he lost the Use of his Reason. (Cervantes 15)

Don Quixote's reading-induced madness famously sparks an entire mock-chivalric romance. Wroth's use of reading as the cause for Antissia's madness is a clear reference to Cervantes's work.

In *Urania 2*, Antissia's nephew, Antissius, makes a connection between his aunt's reading habits and her madness:

> [S]he fell to studdy and got a tuter (O her fill for such a skoller, one who had binn mad in studying how to make a peece of poetrie to excel Ovid, and to bee more admired then hee is). . . . And soe fittly hath he served her as to make her as mad as him self, beeing a dangerous thing att any time for a weake woeman to studdy higher matters then their cappasitie can reach to; and indeed she was butt weake in true sence, butt colorick ever and rash, and now in such a heighth of poetry, which att the best is butt a frency. (*Urania* 2:40.33–41.7)

In other words, Antissia's madness is tied to her reading of poetry.

However, Antissius carefully explains that his aunt's madness is also related to her identity as "a weake woeman" (*Urania* 2:41.4) who studies beyond her "cappasittie" (*Urania* 2:41.5). Such ideas were commonplace in early modern England even among those who promoted women's education. Juan Luis Vives, for instance, advises in *The Education of a Christian Woman* that young women "peruse books that impart instruction and morals."[11] He later describes a fascination with fictional tales of love and war as "madness."[12] In

---

[11] Juan Luis Vives, *The Education of a Christian Woman: A Sixteenth-Century Manual*, ed. and trans. Charles Fantazzi (Chicago: Univ. of Chicago Press, 2000), 71.

[12] Vives, *Education*, 76.

Wroth's own life, Denny explicitly voiced these ideas. His poetic response to *Urania* includes the accusation, "Thy witt runns madd" (Denny line 12) and concludes with the admonition to "leave idle bookes alone / For wise and worthier women have writte none" (Denny lines 25–26).[13] The idea that Wroth's writing makes her less "wise" and "worthy" reflects the same suspicion of women's intellectual activities that pervades Antissius's commentary on his aunt's studies. Thus, the initial descriptions of Antissia's madness suggest that the madness stems from her quixotic study habits, in keeping with the general early modern attitude about reading and its dangers.

However, an additional influence on Antissia's madness beyond her reading of poetry is her tutor. Antissius describes his aunt's tutor as "one who had binn mad in studying how to make a peece of poetrie to excel Ovid, and to bee more admired then hee is" (*Urania* 1:40.35–36). The tutor's madness is important for a few reasons. First, it undermines Antissius's deprecating remarks about female weakness, for this man has also been driven mad through study. Second, it is not the studying of poetry itself, but the man's overweening ambition that drives him mad. Several other poets in *Urania*, including Wroth's protagonist, Pamphilia, remain in possession of their wits throughout the saga. Thus, the tutor's madness is not something that happens to all students of poetry, but it is a result of his pride. Finally, while hiring a mad tutor may be an error in judgment on Antissia's part, the tutor's madness suggests that Antissia's own madness is due not to her reading itself but to the company in which she reads. Most poets in *Urania*, including Antissia herself in an earlier episode, pursue their writing in a solitary manner (see *Urania* 1:114.8–36).[14] Antissia's poor choice of companion is the problem, not her choice to study or her selected reading materials.

---

[13] In one of his letters, dated 26 February [1621], Denny explicitly identifies Wroth's aunt, Mary Sidney Herbert, as such a woman. Denny advises Wroth to "followe the rare, and pious example of your vertuous and learned Aunt, who translated so many godly books and especially the holly psalms of David, that no doubt now shee sings in the quier of Heaven those divine meditations," 239.

[14] For a more "mainstream" example of solitary writing, see Pamphilia's composition of the poem "Heart drops distilling like a new-cut vine"

While Wroth's characters seem content to ignore the tutor's role, her readers must be more astute. Rather than agreeing with early modern theories about the dangers of reading, this episode actually takes a contrary position. Through the character of Antissia's mad tutor, Wroth posits that the wrong kind of study, not the wrong materials, is the problem. Wroth's inclusion of the mad tutor absolves Antissia of much of her blame and suggests that readers themselves (not authors) must make wiser choices about what—and with whom—they read.

Antissia's Poetry: Reading with the Right Attitude

After exploring the causes of Antissia's madness, Wroth moves on to its effects, which, again, seem to be drawn from some of Don Quixote's mad behavior. For instance, Don Quixote dresses in ridiculous armor (Cervantes 16–17) and speaks in "extravagant Conceits . . . in Imitation, and in the very Stile of those, which the reading of Romances had furnish'd him with" (Cervantes 21). Antissia appears in disordered dress ("neither drest, nor undrest," *Urania* 2:33.42) and communicates in what her nephew describes as "raging, raving, extravagant discoursive language" (*Urania* 2:41.11). Like Don Quixote, then, Antissia's dress and speech reflect her madness. However, the lengthiest descriptions of Antissia's madness focus on her creation and recitation of two poems.[15] The first of these poems is addressed to her husband, Dolorindus, who is mightily offended by the verse. The second poem is addressed to a much more sympathetic audience, the wise woman Melissea. Through these two poems and their differing audiences, Wroth again engages with the early modern cultural preoccupation with the dangers of reading. The contrasting reactions of Dolorindus and Melissea make these

---

(*Urania* 1:62). Bernadette Andrea examines this scene in detail in "Pamphilia's Cabinet: Gendered Authorship and Empire in Lady Mary Wroth's *Urania*," *ELH* 38 (2001): 335–58; see also Nona Fienberg, "Mary Wroth's Poetics of the Self," *Studies in English Literature 1500–1800* 42, no. 1 (2002): 121–36; Rebecca Laroche, "Pamphilia Across a Crowded Room: Mary Wroth's Entry into Literary History," *Genre* 30 (1997): 267–88.

[15] Antissia also composes poetry when sane; see *Urania* 1:114.16–29.

two characters examples of bad and good interpretation respectively. These characters are thus sources of instruction for Wroth's own readers.

Antissia's first poem is a love poem addressed to her husband.[16] She says the poem will "shew ... my love in verce" (*Urania* 2:51.8–9). The poem begins by calling on the "lusty gamesters of the sea: / Billowes, waves, and winds" (*Urania* 2:50.16–17) to bear witness to Antissia's love. Incidentally, she and Dolorindus are on a sea voyage in this scene, so the introduction to the poem demonstrates an awareness of her surroundings despite her madness. She goes on to reject Diana's "pale face" (*Urania* 2:50.21) in favor of other classical figures, such as Juno, who better reflect Antissia's feelings. The poem's final stanza, however, focuses on Venus:

> And you, faire starry sky, beeholde
> Venus me commaunds,
> That by noe meanes love showld grow colde
> Butt blowe the fire brands.
> Solls best heat must fill our vaines;
> Thes are true loves highest straines.
> (*Urania* 2:50.34–51.2)

This final stanza uses the commonplace image of fire as love's passion, emphasizing Venus as the superior classical model for love.[17]

Dolorindus, the poem's intended audience, does not appreciate his wife's artistry. He scolds her, saying, "Did ever a chaste lady make such a songe, ore chaste eares indure the hearing itt? Fy, fy, Antissia, if you will write, write sence and modestie, nott this stuff that maides will blush to hear" (*Urania* 2:51.4–7). Dolorindus's scolding is similar to the jibes Denny gave Wroth, particularly Denny's

---

[16] Love, of course, is a primary cause of madness in early modern literature; Wroth uses this concept extensively in *Urania* 1—probably most prominently in the Throne of Love episode, where drinking from an enchanted stream produces "distraction" in several characters, 1:49.27. *Orlando Furioso*, which Roberts notes as influential for Wroth, may provide inspiration for some of the love-madness in *Urania* (Wroth, *The First Part*, xxvii).

[17] One has, of course, only to note Beilin's summary of expectations for early modern women—"obedient, chaste, and silent"—to predict Dolorindus's negative reaction to the elevation of Venus (*Redeeming Eve*, xix).

admonition to "redeeme the tym with writing as large a volume of heavenly layes and holy love as you have of lascivious tales and amorous toyes" (Denny, 239). Both Dolorindus and Denny entreat women to turn their attention to something more (supposedly) appropriate than love and passion.

While Antissia, like Wroth herself, is roundly scolded for writing poetry about passion, it is worth noting that Wroth includes this poem in full. She thus declines to protect her readers from the supposed immodesty of the verse. This suggests that Wroth does not view such poetry as dangerous. In fact, while the quality of Antissia's verse is perhaps not the highest among all the *Urania* poems, the content does not differ widely from Wroth's other poetry. For instance, Wroth's sonnet sequence, *Pamphilia to Amphilanthus*, opens with a poem featuring the same two images Antissia uses here: Venus and love's flame.[18] *Pamphilia to Amphilanthus* 1 describes a dream in which the speaker encounters "bright Venus Queene of love" (Wroth line 6), who presides over a pile of burning hearts. Venus then presents "one hart flaming more then all the rest" (Wroth line 9) to the speaker, putting it in the speaker's breast to symbolize the beginning of her passion for Amphilanthus. If it is Antissia's madness that brought on her passionate poetry, then Pamphilia, Wroth's emblem of pure love, experiences the same madness.

Antissia's poem does not seem to have a negative effect on anyone but Dolorindus; however, Dolorindus's anger has more far-reaching consequences. After Dolorindus finishes his scolding, the narrator says, "With that, as if his angry words storming in him had had congruitie with the seas and winds, a storme rose" (*Urania* 2:51.11–12). In other words, if anyone's words have the power to harm in this story, it is Dolorindus's angry scolding. In this way, Wroth suggests that it is the readers or listeners of poetry who are responsible for any harm that their reading does—not the poet, mad or sane.

Antissia's second "mad" poem is addressed to a more sympathetic audience: the wise woman Melissea, who will eventually effect Antissia's cure. The verses are delivered in a mad manner— the narrator describes Antissia "singing thes Verces and stiring up

---

[18] For this essay, I used the text of *Pamphilia to Amphilanthus* 1 found on page 85 of *The Poems of Lady Mary Wroth*, ed. Roberts.

and downe like an new broke colte in a haulter" (*Urania* 2:51.23–24). However, the poem itself demonstrates a clear understanding of Melissea's power and her capacity to help Antissia. The poem reads:

> This night the Moone eclipsed was
>> Alas,
> Butt quickly she did brightlier shine
>> Devine,
> Prognosticating by sweet raine
> That all things showld bee cleere againe.
>
> Sweet raine foretells us good to growe,
>> And flowe,
> Coole drops, sweet moisture, flower bring
>> To spring,
> Which fruict brings forthe, and soe shall wee
> Live hopefully all good to see.
> Butt in this time the sun is loste
>> And crost,
> Though in Antipides nott quite bereft
>> Nor left,
> Butt in just course shall come againe,
> And with pure light both shine and raigne.
>>>> (*Urania* 2:51.25–52.2)

Antissia's subsequent speech makes clear that Melissea is the sun in the poem, returning after a period of absence. This is an apt description of Melissea, who is a positive character in both halves of *Urania* but appears only at intervals. In addition, both Antissia's cure and the more famous cure of Urania's lovesickness in part 1 (*Urania* 1:230.7–231.10) are accomplished by Melissea through water.[19] The water imagery of the second stanza thus suggests Antissia's awareness of Melissea's power.

Additionally, Melissea's reaction to the poem demonstrates her compassion for Antissia. While recognizing that Antissia is not in

---

[19] This cure provides further comparison with *Don Quixote*, whose madness is said to dry up the "Moisture of his Brain" (Cervantes 15). This reference to dryness suggests that Don Quixote's madness is, in early modern humoral theory, an imbalance—Antissia's madness, cured by water, may have a similar humoral resonance.

her right mind, Melissea does not scold or reprimand, as Dolorindus does. Rather, Melissea acknowledges the sincere compliment Antissia includes in the poem, saying "The honors you give mee are to much for mee to receave" (*Urania* 2:52.17). When Melissea later speaks of the pity Antissia's madness induces, she does so "a little lower" so that her words will not "give offence" (*Urania* 2:52.26). In other words, Melissea is a sympathetic audience who recognizes Antissia's intention (to compliment her hostess). In contrast to Dolorindus, who misinterprets Antissia's expression of love, Melissea recognizes that Antissia's madness does not separate her entirely from reality.

Both of the "mad" poems convey sincere emotions: love, desire, and devotion for Dolorindus; admiration for Melissea. It is the audiences who make these poems have wildly different effects. Dolorindus's anger confuses his wife and may be connected to the great storm that sweeps their ship away. In contrast, Melissea's compassion keeps Antissia from further distress. In fact, it is in Melissea's home that Antissia's madness is cured. Dolorindus and Melissea, then, provide two contrasting models for readers. Despite the fact that Dolorindus's reaction mirrors real-life readers like Denny, it is Melissea whom Wroth presents in this episode as the best example for readers.

Conclusion

Antissia's madness in *Urania* 2 appears, at first, to fulfill early modern anxieties about the dangers of reading. Clearly drawing on *Don Quixote* for the causes and effects of Antissia's madness, the episode also touches on gendered attitudes about women readers and the dangers of study. Through the characters of the mad tutor and Melissea, however, Wroth uses this episode to critique such attitudes. In particular, Melissea is the ideal reader in this episode, because she understands the meaning of Antissia's words, takes no offense, and offers a solution to Antissia's distress. Wroth's ultimate model for readers, possibly reflecting her own real-life problems with readers like Denny, is thus one of generosity and careful interpretation.

Although Wroth does not ultimately participate in early modern concerns about the dangers of reading, *Urania* is not without connection to larger concerns in early modern print culture. As Sarah Rodgers notes, *Urania* as a whole bridges coterie and print circulation, itself a living illustration of the ways in which the relationship between authors and readers changed during the early modern era.[20] Similarly, Wroth's portrayal of reading in the episode of Antissia's madness may anticipate the anti-censorship rhetoric of texts such as Milton's *Areopagitica*, which argues that readers, not governments or publishers, should decide what knowledge is valuable.[21] In other words, *Urania* (in general) and the Antissia episode in *Urania* 2 (in particular) contribute to the changing conception of reading in the early modern period. Chief among its contributions is Wroth's use of Antissia's reading-related madness, along with the reactions of characters such as Antissius, Dolorindus, and Melissea, to critique poor readers and—most importantly—to model the type of generous, compassionate, and interpretive reading that Wroth wants her own best readers to practice.

North Greenville University

---

[20] Sarah Rodgers, "Embedded Poetry and Coterie Readers in Mary Wroth's *Urania*," *Studies in Philology* 111, no. 3 (Summer 2014): 470–85.

[21] John Milton, *Areopagitica*, in *John Milton: The Major Works*, ed. Stephen Orgel and Jonathan Goldberg (Oxford: Oxford Univ. Press, 1991), 236–72.

"Thou thyself likewise art lyttle made": Spenser, Catullus, and the Aesthetics of "smale poemes"

Melissa J. Rack

S PENSER'S late-career pastorals feature several charming insect-protagonists who demonstrate lyric smallness within an epic milieu. *Virgil's Gnat* (1591) frames an inset lament with a surprisingly vast allusive scope. As Ronald Bond explains, the Gnat's complaint "touches on tragic figures such as Sisyphus and Tantalus, enduring punishment in Tartarus, various chaste women (Alcestis, Penelope, Eurydice) who epitomize heroic love, [and] military heroes from both sides of the Trojan War (Hector, Ajax, Achilles, etc.)."[1] In *Muiopotmos* (1591), an equally tiny butterfly is augmented as a small-scale Achilles armed for battle in a mini-ekphrasis that, as William Oram explains, "burlesques epic convention."[2] Similarly, in the verses known as "the Anacreontics," which mark the transition between the *Amoretti* and the *Epithalamion*, a "gentle Bee with his loud trumpet murm'ring" (line 25) mischievously stings baby

---

[1] Ronald Bond, "Introduction to *Virgil's Gnat*," in *The Yale Edition of the Shorter Poems of Edmund Spenser*, ed. William A. Oram (New Haven, CT: Yale Univ. Press, 1989), 294.

[2] Edmund Spenser, "Muiopotmos," in *The Yale Edition of the Shorter Poems of Edmund Spenser*, ed. William A. Oram (New Haven, CT: Yale Univ. Press, 1989), 415n56. This epic encounter between the butterfly Clarion and the spider Aragnoll is framed as a "dolorous debate . . . / Betwixt two mightie ones of great estate" (1, 3).

Cupid as he slumbers.[3] Cupid is infantilized as "little Cupid" and "Venus baby," in lines which relate his confrontation with an equally tiny mock-epic adversary: a "beast so small" who "flyes about / and threatens all with corage stout." As Cupid complains of this injustice, Venus reminds him of his own smallness, which stands in contrast to the vast dominion he sustains over the hearts of lovers, both human and divine: "See thou thy selfe likewise art lyttle made / . . . And yet thou suffrest neyther gods in sky, / nor men in earth to rest" (lines 35, 37–38).

Spenser's attention to smallness in these poems indicates a curious preoccupation with the miniature. In this essay, I propose that this impulse to miniaturize is a Neo-Alexandrian or *neoteric* signature, and Spenser's revision of a distinctly Catullan stylistic, formerly manifest in its original Latin context as a fondness for diminutives.[4] As the Catullan diminutive in turn evokes the Alexandrian epic miniature, this strategic miniaturization sheds particular light on the seeming aesthetic disjunction in Spenser's late career shift from epic to lyric composition. Alongside these tiny tropes, the lyric impulse to miniaturize is similarly manifest via narrative and paratextual framing. Indeed, Spenser's paratextual apparatus often disrupts narrative continuity, miniaturizing as it reframes the narrative sequentially (as in the "Anacreontics," *Astrophel*, and *The Shepheardes Calender*), as a self-conscious unfinished fragment (as in *The Cantos of Mutabilitie*), or as one of several "smale poemes" or "parcels" (as in *The Complaints*).[5] As such, Spenser's quasi-meditations on the miniature denote an aesthetic that is as much structural as

---

[3] Edmund Spenser, "[Anacreontics]," in *The Yale Edition*. All quotations in this essay from Spenser's shorter poems are excerpted from this edition, unless otherwise specified.

[4] The aesthetic I describe in this essay applies to the following poems: *The Complaints* (1591); *Daphnaïda* (1591); *Colin Clouts Come Home Againe* (1595); *Astrophel* (1595); the verses known as "the Anacreontics" (1595); and the *Two Cantos of Mutabilitie* (1609). Other methods of miniaturization include paratextual interruptions—spacing, ornamental borders, etc. that break up the narrative.

[5] For a fuller discussion of paratext, see Gerard Genette, *Paratexts: Thresholds of Interpretation*, trans. Jane E. Lewin (Cambridge: Cambridge Univ. Press).

stylistic, as these poems further distill their epic contexts via allusion in sub-narratives that mirror their larger narratives.

Spenser's concern with the miniature also suggests an interiority, self-consciousness, or poetic introspection, as the plaintive aspect of these tiny tropes invokes a poetic form marked by its self-reflexive nature. As Spenser concedes in the *Epithalamion*, complaints are poems in which the Muses "mourne" their "owne mishaps."[6] Patrick Cheney, addressing Spenser's problematic deviation from the *rota Virgilii* in his late career return to pastoral, maintains that Spenser's 1590's pastorals are anomalous precisely because complaint as a form is a "genre about genre" within which Spenser "typologically enfolds" diverse genres in order to define and distinguish their difference.[7] Interestingly, from the outset, the paratext of the *The Complaints* volume announces the poems within it are "smale." William Ponsonbie's preface, "The Printer to the *Gentle Reader*," places noteworthy emphasis on size:

> Since my late setting foorth of the *Faerie Queene* ... I have sithence endevoured ... to get into my hands such smale Poemes of the same Authors; ... I have by good meanes gathered together

---

[6] Edmund Spenser, "Epithalamion," in *The Yale Edition*, 662.

[7] Richard Helgerson and Patrick Cheney have struggled to situate these poems in the arc of the *rota Virgilii*, with varying success. Spenser alludes to the *rota Virgilii* in lines 1–4 of the first book of *The Faerie Queene*, imitating proem lines in Renaissance editions of Virgil's *Aeneid*. See A. C. Hamilton, *The Faerie Queene*, by Edmund Spenser (London: Longman, 2001), 29n, stanza 1. For perspectives on career criticism, see Patrick Cheney, *Spenser's Famous Flight: A Renaissance Idea of a Literary Career* (Toronto, ON: Univ. of Toronto Press, 1993); and Richard Helgerson, *Self-Crowned Laureates: Spenser, Jonson, Milton and the Literary System* (Berkeley: Univ. of California Press, 1983). For problems with this model, see David Scott Wilson-Okamura, "Problems in the Virgilian Career" *Spenser Studies* 26 (2011). Wilson-Okamura cites several factors, including the absence of a georgic equivalent, Spenser's lack of an adequate laureate pension, the length of *The Faerie Queene* itself, and Spenser's play with sexual topoi. Cheney, *Spenser's Famous Flight*, 47–48. Cheney explains that Spenser "folds georgic into pastoral to define pastoral; he folds georgic and pastoral into epic to define epic; he folds georgic, pastoral, love lyric, and epic into hymn to define hymn," etc.

these few parcels present . . . praying you . . . graciouslie to enter-
taine the new Poet.[8]

Although Ponsonbie alleges to have mastery over the volume's
compilation, Oram asserts the "discrete title pages and separate
dedications" reveal "it is [more] likely Spenser himself had a hand
in publishing the volume."[9] It is not far-fetched, then, to imagine
Ponsonbie ventriloquizing uniquely Spenserian concerns within
the preface. This fashioning of these poems as "smale," and one of
a "few parcels," both underscores their generic distinctiveness and
implies a certain rusticity or mutability of form—the fragmentari-
ness of scattered pieces integral to a larger whole. "Parcel" in the
sixteenth century denotes a "part, portion, or division *of* something
. . . a small part," hence implying the verse in *The Complaints* is
both small in scale and a fragment of some larger unspecified narrative.[10] Ponsonbie's allusion to Spenser as the "new Poet" reminds
us his lyric ventures tend to be forays into the avant-garde.[11]

It is with a similar authorial pronouncement of the smallness,
insignificance, and newness of one's verse that Catullus opens his
libellus (small book).[12] In it, he espouses a commitment to innovation that is arguably analogous to Spenser's. It is because of the stylistic eccentricity of this innovation that Cicero groups him among

---

[8] Edmund Spenser, "The Printer to the Gentle Reader," in *Complaints*,
Renascence Editions, ed. Risa S. Bear (Eugene: Univ. of Oregon Press,
1996). This html e-text of the *Complaints* was prepared from Alexander B.
Grosart's *The Complete Works in Verse and Prose of Edmund Spenser* [1882]
and from Ernest de Sélincourt's *Spenser's Minor Poems* [Oxford, 1910],
www.luminarium.org/renascence-editions/complaints.html.

[9] William A. Oram, "Introduction to *Complaints*," in *The Yale Edition*,
217.

[10] "Parcel," *The Oxford English Dictionary Online*, accessed May 30,
2018.

[11] E.K., "Epistle to *The Shepheardes Calender* (1579)," in *The Yale Edition*, 13.

[12] [Small book]. For a persona-driven poet like Catullus the notion of
poetic insignificance is surely tongue-in-cheek. Catullus certainly did not
consider himself, or his verse, insignificant.

the avant-garde poets he names "neoterics" or "the new poets."[13] *Catullus 1* serves as opening poem, dedication, and aesthetic declaration: "Cui dono lepidum nouum libellum / Arida modo pumice expolitum? . . ." [Who's the dedicatee of my new witty / small book, fresh-polished with abrasive? . . .] (1–2).[14] The diminutive (*libellum* and *libelli* for *liber* [book]) is a hallmark of Catullan style; hence, the diminutive's ability to place emphasis on smallness implies its centrality to a Catullan aesthetic.[15] As Julia Haig Gaisser explains, "*Lepidus* [wit] and *novus* [new] are catch-words in the neoteric vocabulary; *expolitum* [polish] puns on the polish given the papyrus roll and that applied to its contents by the artful poet; [and] the diminutive *libellus* announces that Catullus plans a work on a small (i.e., Alexandrian) scale."[16] As Catullus's aesthetic models are the Alexandrian scholar-poets of the 3rd century BCE, namely Callimachus (310/305–240 BCE) and Theocritus (c. 300–260 BCE), Catullus fashions his verse by the same "slender muse" Callimachus espouses in the prologue to his *Aetia*.[17]

---

[13] Also [the younger ones, the innovators]. Peter Green, "Introduction: The Literary Context," in *The Poems of Catullus*, trans. Peter Green (Berkeley: Univ. of California Press, 2005), 11. Also see R.O.A.M Lyne, "The Neoteric Poets," in *The Latin Love Poets: From Catullus to Horace* (New York: Oxford Univ. Press, 1980).

[14] Gaius Valerius Catullus, *The Poems of Catullus*, 45. All bracketed translations of Catullus in this essay are Green's, unless otherwise specified.

[15] [Little book] is the diminutive of [book].

[16] *Lepidus* [wit], *nouum* [new], and *expolitum* [polish]. Julia Haig Gaisser, *Catullus and His Renaissance Readers* (Oxford: Clarendon Press, 1993), 4.

[17] *Aetia* means "origins, or causes." The "slender muse" is quoted from the following lines: "καὶ γὰρ ὅτε πρώτιστον ἐμοῖς ἐπὶ δέλτον ἔθηκα / γούνασιν, Ἀπ[ό]λλων εἶπεν ὅ μοι Λύκιος / '. . . . . . .]. . . ἀοιδέ, τὸ μὲν θύος ὅττι πάχιστον / θρέψαι, τὴ]ν Μοῦσαν δ' ὠγαθὲ λεπταλέην / πρὸς δέ σε] καὶ τόδ' ἄνωγα, τὰ μὴ πατέουσιν ἅμαξαι / τὰ στείβειν, ἑτέρων ἴχνια μὴ καθ' ὁμά." [. . . poet, raise your sacrificial victim as fat as possible, / but, good man, keep your Muse slender; / and this too I ask (of you), walk a path unbeaten by wagons, / don't drive your chariot along the common ruts of others / nor upon a wide road, but (on) unworn / tracks, even if you will be driving more narrow (ones)." Callimachus, *Callimachus: Aetia*, trans. Susan Stephens (Carlisle, PA: Dickinson College Commentaries, 2015).

πολλάκ]ι μοι Τελχῖνες ἐπιτρύζουσιν ἀοιδῇ,
νήιδες οἳ Μούσης οὐκ ἐγένοντο φίλοι,
εἵνεκεν οὐχ ἓν ἄεισμα διηνεκὲς ἢ βασιλ[η
. . . . .]ας ἐν πολλαῖς ἤνυσα χιλιάσιν
ἢ . . . . .] . ους ἥρωας, ἔπος δ᾽ ἐπὶ τυτθὸν ελ[
παῖς ἅτε, τῶν δ᾽ ἐτέων ἡ δεκὰς οὐκ ὀλίγη.

[Often the Telchines grumble at my poetry
(ignorant, they weren't born friends of the Muse)
because I did not complete a single continuous poem
in many thousands of lines either on kings ... or on heroes,
but, like a child, I ... work (?) on a small scale
though the decades of my years are not few]. (1–5)[18]

Here Callimachus champions the "big book, big evil" precept for which he is known by juxtaposing verse that is lengthy and pretentious (historical epic) and short and refined (lyric).

The Alexandrian commitment to small-scale epic revision is thought to have inspired the classical *epyllion*, or minor epic, the formal exemplar of which is Callimachus's narrative poem *Hecale*, alongside *Catullus 64*.[19] While *epyllion* is a relatively modern term, it usefully distinguishes a small-scale poem that miniaturizes epic narrative within a conspicuously lyric form, reframing selections from Homeric myth, preserving epic language and convention, and focusing on the idiosyncratic experiences of the individu-

---

www.dcc.dickinson.edu/callimachus-aetia/prologue-against-telchines. All Greek translations are Stephens's, unless otherwise specified.

[18] Stephens's note reads as follows: "Callimachus begins by defending himself against his critics, whom he labels "Telchines." The Telchines were mythological figures, sorcerers or magicians, who became hateful to the gods, and whom Zeus or Apollo obliterated. The Florentine Scholia (lines 3–8) identify the Telchines with a few of Callimachus's contemporaries, most notably the epigrammatists Asclepiades and Posidippus. But despite ancient and modern speculation, it is not certain if Telchines refers to real individuals or is a fictional adversary."

[19] For a discussion of Alexandrian aesthetics via *Hecale*, see A. S. Hollis, *Callimachus: Hecale* (New York: Oxford Univ. Press, 1990); and Peter E. Knox, "Catullus and Callimachus," in *A Companion to Catullus*, ed. Marilyn B. Skinner (Hoboken, NJ: Blackwell, 2007). Knox names Callimachus's *Hecale*, the *Hermes* of Eratosthenes, Theocritus's *Idylls* 13 ("Hylas") and 24 ("Heracliscus") as characteristically Alexandrian epyllia.

al.[20] To comprehend Spenser's debt to Catullus, we must first reimagine his later pastorals as epyllia. *Muiopotmos*, for example, is widely considered an epyllion in critical discussions of the genre.[21] Cheney argues we should read *Colin Clout* as an epyllion, and both Andrew Zurcher and Humphrey Tonkin have proposed that *The Mutabilitie Cantos* is a freestanding epyllion.[22] Furthermore, placement of "the Anacreontics" before the *Epithalamion* suggests these verses might be formally classified in a similar manner. Critics have long acknowledged the themes and structures of Spenser's *Epithalamion* imitate the marriage-songs of Catullus. Alongside *C.61* and *C.62*, *Catullus 64* (also called "The Marriage of Peleus and Thetis") is framed as an epithalamium; however, the poem is also an epyllion. If Spenser referred to this poem as a model for the *Epithalamion*, *C.64* provides a curious context for the composition of "the Anacreontics." If reconsidered as a continuous narrative that is self-consciously fragmented (made sequential by the paratext), "the

---

[20] For an excellent discussion of the genre, Marco Fantuzzi and Richard Hunter, "Chapter 5: Epic in a Minor Key," in *Tradition and Innovation in Hellenistic Poetry* (Cambridge: Cambridge Univ. Press, 2004), 191–245.

[21] See Clark Hulse, *Metamorphic Verse: The Elizabethan Minor Epic* (Princeton, NJ: Princeton Univ. Press, 1981), 3. Hulse names *Muiopotmos* in the opening lines of the introduction to his book on the genre.

[22] See Patrick Cheney, *Colin Clouts Come Home Againe, Astrophel, and the Doleful Lay of Clorinda (1595)*, in *The Oxford Handbook of Edmund Spenser*, ed. Richard A. MacCabe (New York: Oxford Univ. Press, 2010, 241. Cheney writes "By re-classifying *Colin Clout* as a pastoral epyllion, we gain access to its fundamental bridging role in Spenser's literary career, for the 'minor epic was . . . the proving ground for . . . epic,' a form 'above the pastoral. . . . and below the epic, the transition between the two in the *gradus Vergilianus*' (Hulse 1981:12)." Humphrey Tonkin, *The Faerie Queene* (New York: Routledge, 1989), 43–44. Tonkin writes of "The air of completeness" in the *Cantos*, and suggests "It is a useful exercise to imagine the shorter work and to consider how we might justify reading [them] as a finished whole." Andrew Zurcher, "The Printing of the Cantos of Mutabilitie in 1609," in *Celebrating Mutabilitie: Essays on Edmund Spenser's Mutabilitie Cantos* (Manchester: Manchester Univ. Press, 2010). Zurcher argues that the printer Matthew Lownes prepared the 1609 edition from a 1596 copy that Spenser had planned for publication in its independent form; thus, Spenser had intended the poem as an independent work.

Anacreontics" might be better understood as a micro-epyllion, an epyllion of which smallness is its narrative subject, or as a series of micro-epyllia, in which form reflects content. Nevertheless, these stanzas distill a miniaturizing impulse that likewise characterizes Spenser's lyric aesthetic, and as such, they are themselves a statement of aesthetic miniaturization in miniature.[23]

It is Catullus's privileging of the finely wrought, small-scale poem as a better kind of epic that informs Spenser's structural miniaturization via the inset narrative, which is both a formal characteristic and a uniquely Catullan technique.[24] In his study of the Elizabethan epyllion, Clark Hulse explains the form's interior narratives are both allusion and emblem, "mov[ing] back and forth by analogy among the semi-independent portions of the narrative, depending upon the reader to respond" and recall the allusion, or interpret "the codified allegorical significance of mythological image."[25] Often, these inset narratives are developed via elaborate "complaint frames, by ekphrastic digression, and . . . by the amplification of character through apostrophe."[26] *Catullus 64*, for example, frames Ariadne's seaside lament for her departed lover Theseus.[27]

---

[23] Interestingly, nearly all of the most significant poets and dramatists of the 1590's wrote epyllia, as the work of Jim Ellis, Clark Hulse, and William Keach has illustrated; hence the form emerged as a fashionable trend during the 1590's, particularly among young men at the Inns of Court. See Hulse, *Metamorphic Verse*; Jim Ellis, *Sexuality and Citizenship: Metamorphosis an Elizabethan Erotic Verse* (Toronto, ON: Toronto Univ. Press, 2003); and William Keach, *Elizabethan Erotic Narratives* (New Brunswick, NJ: Rutgers Univ. Press, 1977).

[24] Hulse, *Metamorphic Verse*, 24. Hulse explains, "[These poems] characteristically use digression and inset narrative, working toward meaning through analogy, recollection and juxtaposition . . . so that a single spinoff episode tends to reproduce in miniature the structural principle of the whole work."

[25] Ibid.

[26] Ibid., 25.

[27] As the source of Dido's lament in Virgil's *Aeneid*, Ariadne's complaint is an oft-unrecognized point of origin for the Elizabethan complaint. Catullus 64 predates *The Aeneid*, Ovid's *Heroides* and *Mirror for Magistrates*. The complaint is often indistinguishable from the Elizabethan epyllion.

Through Ariadne, Catullus recalls and iconizes a portrait of longing by representing a character as a trope, for Ariadne is herself a crafted art-object; her plaint is an ekphrastic digression, an image adorning the wedding coverlet which "heroum mira uirtutes indicat arte [portrays in marvelous art the brave deeds of heroes]" (lines 50–51). We know her portrait is meant to be visually consumed, for the narrator conflates Ariadne's loss with the loss of her clothing as she is undressed by the wind. While her sexualization amplifies the representation of her longing, it also moves the reader towards the exterior of the in-set frame as it calls attention to the gaze.[28] In this way, the artistry of Ariadne's portrait participates in the poem's formal intricacy, reflecting in turn the narrative's concern with poetic artistry, for *C.64* is a poem that narrates the revision, re-crafting, and miniaturization of a larger, communal narrative.

Similarly, Spenser's inset narratives are often figured as portraits of wailing women. *The Ruines of Time* opens thus: "I did behold / A Woman sitting sorrowfullie wailing, / Rending her yeolow locks" (lines 8–9). *Tears of the Muses* is structured as a procession of plaintive portraits, linked by visual and auditory descriptions of each individual Muse-figure. *Astrophel* mirrors this interlocking structure, in which "the doleful Lay of Clorinda" functions as an inset narrative, followed by a series of elegies that feature diverse authorial voices, the transition from the voice of Spenser's poem mediated by the ambiguity of the Lay's authorship. Comparably, in *Daphnaïda*, the narrator is alone, meditating on "this worlds vainnesse and lifes wretchednesse" (line 34), when his psychological state is mirrored by Alcyon, who is feminized in his intemperate grief, in a plaint (lines 71–539) that is arguably both primary narrative and inset narrative. In turn, Alcyon's lament frames an anti-lament (lines 263–92) through which Daphne's ghost intimates the possibility of consolation, but instead only affirms his despair:

---

[28] The breast imagery suggested by the diction is particularly striking "non contecta leui uelatum pectus amictu, / non tereti strophio lactentis uincta papillas / omnia quae toto delapsa e corpore passim. [Lost the light garment veiling her torso, lost the / rounded breast-band that gathered her milk white bosom— / all of them, slipped from her body every which way]" (lines 64–66).

Our daies are full of dolor and disease,
Our life afflicted with incessant paine,
That nought on earth may lessen or appease
Why then should I desire here to remaine?
(lines 274–77)

Daphne's affirmation sustains Spenser's deviation from formal elegy (as anti-elegy), mirroring both primary narrative and poetic form.[29]

Apart from critical acknowledgment that *C.64* served as a model for Spenser's *Epithalamium*, the influence of Catullus on Spenser has long been understood as minimal; yet, Catullus was a darling for imitation on the continent. The French Pleiades' fondness for Catullus would not have escaped Spenser's notice. As Gaisser explains, "Du Bellay called for the adoption of the Catullan hendecasyllable into French poetry as early as 1549, but the [Paris lectures of Marc-Antoine Muret on Catullus] provided the essential stimulus, inspiring not only Ronsard but other French poets as well to write in the Catullan manner."[30] Accordingly, Ronsard's *Livret de folastries* (1553) bears a dedication to "A Janot Parisien" (i.e., Jean-Antoine de Baïf) which mimics *Catullus 1*. Ronsard writes, "To whom do I give these trifles and these dainty little verses? . . . To you, my friend Janot. . . . Take it then, Janot, such as it is . . . so that you and I and my book may live more than a single age."[31] Furthermore, both Gaisser and Alex Wong have established that the revival of Catullan motifs in Neo-Latin poetry was an early sixteenth-century vogue.[32]

---

[29] *Daphnaïda*'s lack of consolation has baffled critics for some time now. See William A. Oram, "Introduction to Daphnaïda," in *The Yale Edition*, 490; and David Lee Miller, "Laughing at Spenser's Daphnaïda," *Spenser Studies* 26 (2011): 241. For a discussion of the poem as anti-elegy, see R. Clifton Spargo, *The Ethics of Mourning: Grief and Responsibility in Elegiac Literature* (Baltimore: Johns Hopkins Univ. Press, 2004).

[30] Gaisser, *Catullus and His Renaissance Readers*, 150.

[31] Ronsard, quoted in Gaisser, *Catullus and His Renaissance Readers*, 150.

[32] Gordon Braden, "Catullus," in *The Spenser Encyclopedia*, ed. A. C. Hamilton, et al (Toronto, ON: Univ. of Toronto Press, 1990), 137–38. Braden's entry for "Catullus" calls him a "minor figure" in Spenser's work. For discussions of Catullan imitation in the Renaissance, see Gaisser, *Catullus and His Renaissance Readers*; and Alex Wong, *The Poetry of Kissing in Early Modern Europe* (Cambridge: D. S. Brewer, 2017). Catullan motifs

This trend sheds particular light on Spenser's exposure to Catullus for, as Lee Piepho confirmed in 2002, Spenser owned a book of Neo-Latin poetry: a 1563 edition of *Poëmata*, by the German poet Georgius Sabinus (1508–60), originally bound with the verse of a second Neo-Latinist, Petrus Lotichius Secundus (1528–60).[33] Piepho speculates that Spenser was particularly fond of the latter, for on the final pages of the volume he transcribed a letter, written by a pupil of Lotichius. Within that letter, in Spenser's handwriting, is an excerpt from *Catullus 50*, which reads: "scribens versiculos uterque nostrum / ludebat numero modo hoc modo illoc" [each alternately scribbling little squiblets / playing around with every kind of meter.] (lines 7–8). This autograph manuscript tells us, as Piepho has established, that Spenser read Neo-Latin poetry and, as Piepho's reading of the *Shepheardes Calender* suggests, that it influenced his work, but what it also offers is the only known definitive historical evidence that Spenser read Catullus—or at least two lines of his poetry.

While we can speculate that Spenser was familiar with *Catullus 50*, and perhaps even its companion poem, *Catullus 51*, I propose that even if Spenser had encountered only these two lines, he would still have associated "smallness" with a Catullan aesthetic.[34] The key here is *versiculos* (*versiculus*) a diminutive of *versus*.[35] In the larger

---

include the lyrical kiss from *Catullus 5* and *7*, and the sparrow from *Catullus 2* and *3*. For a useful overview of Neo-Latin poetry in the Renaissance, see Victoria Moul, "Contexts for Latin Verse: Latin and Vernacular." *Neo-Latin Poetry, 1500–1700: An English Perspective*, Oxford Handbooks Online, updated June 2016.

[33] This volume is currently housed at the Folger Shakespeare Library. On the title page is inscribed Spenser's pseudonym "Immerito," and on the final pages Spenser had transcribed three texts in his own hand: two poems and a letter concerning the work of Petrus Lotichius Secundus (1528–60). See Lee Piepho, "The Shepheardes Calender and Neo-Latin Pastoral: A Book Newly Discovered to Have Been Owned by Spenser," *Spenser Studies* 16 (2002): 17–86.

[34] Catullus 50 and 51 are linked via topos and narrative. See John F. Finamore, "Catullus 50 and 51: Friendship, Love, and 'Otium,'" *The Classical World* 78, no. 1 (Sept.–Oct., 1984), 11–19.

[35] *Versiculus* [small verse]; *versus* [a line, row, line of verse, or line of writing].

poem, which details a poetry writing game, *versiculus* refers to fragments of poetry, pieces of a larger whole, or what Ponsonbie would
name "parcels." The word is the same as the one Catullus uses in
16, in which he threatens to bugger Aurelius and Furius in defense
of his "versiculis," which they charge are unmanly because of their
concern with "milia multa basiorum" [countless, thousand kisses].[36]
This reference in the transcribed letter suggests *Catullus 5* (the kiss
poem) is also a *versiculus*; thus, a *versiculus* is both a poem about
love, and something small. Catullus is likely referring to the shorter
poems in the *libellus*—the polymetrics—the *numero modo hoc modo
illoc* [Poems in every kind of meter]. At the same time, the term
versiculus, as literally a fragment of a line of poetry and an uber-
diminutive, functions as an Alexandrian marker. In its celebration
of the tiny, this Neo-Alexandrian poetic value emphasizes, just as
Callimachus did in the *Aetia*, quality over quantity—crafted-ness
over expansiveness.

Certainly if Spenser was familiar with Neo-Latin poetry, as this
manuscript suggests, he would have encountered a certain type of
Catullan imitation widespread among contemporary Neo-Lati-
nists, notably permutations of kisses and sparrows. In this context,
Spenser's "Anacreontics" again assert their significance as neoteric
markers, for that same genre features a distinctly Catullan version of
Anacreontic imitation. The poetic fusion of Anacreon and Catullus
can be traced to the work of Johannes Secundus (1511–36) an early
and influential practitioner of the Basia, or kiss poem, derived in
part from the "milia multa basiorum" of *C.16*. As Wong has detailed
in his recent study of the Basia genre, Secundus played a critical
role in that genre's development; yet, he shaped his permutations of
this Catullan motif with a distinctly Anacreontic flair. Stefan Tilg
explains that the eighth poem in his extremely popular collection
Basia (posthumously published in 1539) "anticipates a number of
stylistic devices characteristic of later Neo-Latin . . . translations and

---

[36] Lines 12–13 read "vos, quod milia multa basiorum / legistis, male
me marem putatis? or Just because you've read about my countless thousand kisses, you think I'm less than virile?" 16 goes on to detail the Catullan aphorism from which is derived (via Martial) the idea that a poet may
be chaste although his verses are not (a notion oft-repeated in Catullan
imitations).

imitations of [the *Carmina Anacreontea*]."[37] While he remarks that these stylistic idiosyncrasies feature anaphora alongside "slightly varied parallelisms," Secundus "combines those features with diminutives[, which] are not a striking characteristic of [the *Carmina Anacreontea*] at all."[38] According to Tilg, subsequent kiss poetry that imitated Secundus followed suit in its fusion of Catullus and Anacreon.[39]

Given the unique fusion of Catullus and Anacreon in Spenser's day, it is likely that the poetic curiosity with anacreontic verse during the sixteenth century was similarly associated with Catullan practice. David Lee Miller suggests that "For Spenser, Anacreontic verse was at once ancient and avant-garde." As the extensive commentary that accompanied Henri Estienne's influential 1554 edition of the *Carmina Anacreontea*, "focused on the theory and practice of literary translation and imitation," the volume emerged "as a kind of laboratory for experimentation with central issues of Renaissance poetics."[40] In both Catullan and Anacreontic imitation, poets were at the forefront of a movement that heralded new advances in poetic practice. In this way, such imitation invited self-conscious reflection. In Spenser's Catullan epithalamium, the poet seemingly pauses to reflect on his own craft of miniaturiza-

---

[37] The *Carmina Anacreontea* was a collection of 60 short imitations of Anacreon's verse represented by Estienne (perhaps unknowingly) as the ancient poet's original work. Stefan Tilg explains that before this publication, Anacreon "was mainly known through ancient testimonies and the two poems found in the *Anthologia Planudea* (1494), a text widely circulated among Renaissance humanists. Tilg writes, "The manuscript Anthologia Palatina, though used by Estienne and possibly being his only source for CA, eluded most scholars of the 16th century and was not finally published until the 19th century" (Tilg footnote 3). See Stefan Tilg, "Neo-Latin Anacreontic Poetry: Its Shape and Its Significance," in *Imitate Anacreon! Mimesis, Poiesis, and Poetic Inspiration in the Carmina Anacreontea*, ed. Manuel Baumbach, Nicola Dummler, and Helmut Grasser (Berlin, Germany: De Gruyter, 2014), 163–254; here 168–69.

[38] Ibid.

[39] Ibid, 164.

[40] David Lee Miller, "Anacreontics Commentary," in *The Collected Works of Edmund Spenser*, ed. David Lee Miller, Patrick Cheney, Joseph Lowenstein, Elizabeth Fowler, and Andrew Zurcher (forthcoming).

tion. Addressing the bride in verses that echo his "Anacreontics," he writes, "an hundred little winged loves . . . Shall fly and flutter round about your bed, / And in the secret darke, . . . / Their prety stealthes shal worke, and snares shal spread" (lines 357–63). These "little winged loves" are tiny flights of fancy, but they are also "amoretti." In these lines, Spenser offers a miniaturized representation of genre framed within the Catullan milieu of his marriage song, giving epic wings to lyric fancy, as they work the "stealthes" and "snares" of the neoteric miniature.

Spenser's tiny tropes and the intricacies of his narrative framing rehearse a number of Neo-Alexandrian tenets, notably reiterations of the values of *expolitum* [polish] and *lepidus* [wit] set forth in *Catullus 1*.[41] As Judith Dundas notes in her discussion of *Muiopotmos*, Spenser's epyllia portray a polished world of art, in which "the mutable world of earthly beauty gives way to the immutable world of artistic beauty," as the poet's mock-heroic insect protagonists evoke "the decorative value of insects in Elizabethan embroideries" to reinforce the artistic value of poetry itself.[42] The ability of Spenser's tiny tropes to successfully navigate both epic and lyric draws on the unique convergence of tradition and innovation that made Alexandrian poetry such an intriguing model for Catullus in the first place, for therein is a celebration of both artistry and wit.

If epic depends on divine inspiration, as the traditional epic invocation suggests, and the *lepidus* and *expolitum* of lyric are accomplished via a learned skill set, as Marco Fantuzzi and Richard Hunter assert, "in their combination of these two series of figures . . . poets turned to their advantage the distinction between inspiration by the poetic divinities, on the one hand, and the primacy of 'craft,' *technē*, on the other." For the aesthetics of newness that informs both Catullus's *libellus* and the lyric experiments of the New Poet these "two [sources of inspiration] . . . formed a powerful

---

[41] *Expolitum* [polish] and *Lepidus* [wit]. Both terms generally refer to craft—conspicuous stylistic ornamentation, displays of erudition, etc.

[42] Judith Dundas, "'Muiopotmos': A World of Art," *The Yearbook of English Studies* 5 (1975): 30–38; here 37. For a discussion of insects in Elizabethan embroidery, see also Joan Evans, *Nature in Design* (London: Oxford Univ. Press, 1933), 98.

unit, no longer . . . opposed."[43] In this neoteric method, this simultaneous shrinking and reimagining of the vastness of Homeric epic in lyric form, Spenser both reframes lyric as a selection from epic, and recasts epic as a function of lyric, realizing new possibilities for epic innovation and at the same time reimagining a national, collective narrative that also privileges the individual and idiosyncratic nature of the stories that comprise that narrative.

University of South Carolina, Salkehatchie

---

[43] Marco Fantuzzi and Richard Hunter, *Tradition and Innovation in Hellenistic Poetry* (Cambridge: Cambridge Univ. Press, 2004,) 1.

The *ordo salutis*: Sacred Circularities in John Donne's "Good Friday 1613. Riding Westward"

Nathan Dixon

JOHN Donne's "Good Friday, 1613. Riding Westward"[1] opens with an elaborate conceit that asks the reader, in what Thomas Sloane calls "the language of a geometrical theorem" to imagine the inner workings of man's soul as a Ptolemaic Universe where devotion should be the prime mover.[2] The speaker in this poem appears to be the same as the speaker in Donne's "Holy Sonnets," a stand-in for the poet himself, and also, according to Sloane, a

---

I would like to thank Dr. John Wall for reviewing an early draft of this paper and for suggesting a variety of secondary sources that have helped determine the drift of my argument. I would also like to thank Dr. Jim Pearce for his help in revising this paper and his patience in listening to me rehearse it. A slightly different version of this paper was given at the Huntington Library in June, 2016.

[1] John Donne, "Good Friday, 1613. Riding Westward," in *The Norton Anthology of English Literature*, 8th ed., vol. 1, ed. Stephen Greenblatt and M. H. Abrams (New York: Norton, 2006), 1299–1300. All other quotations from Donne's poetry come from this edition unless otherwise noted. For a thorough background on the poem and its critical treatment, see: A. B. Chambers, "'Goodfriday, 1613. Riding Westward' the Poem and the Tradition," *ELH* 28, no. 1 (1961): 31–53. For a critical treatment of the general trend of criticism following this particular essay, see: Richard Strier, "Going in the Wrong Direction: Lyric Criticism and Donne's 'Goodfriday, 1613. Riding Westward,'" *George Herbert Journal* 29, no. 1–2 (2005): 13–27.

[2] Thomas O. Sloane, *Donne, Milton, and the End of Humanist Rhetoric* (Berkley: Univ. of California Press, 1985), 37.

stand-in for the Roman god Janus, a two-faced deity, "a juxtaposition, of two directions" whose very being "suggests multiple, even
incongruous perspectives, looking backward and forward" simultaneously.[3] Sloane argues that "the speaker experiences pulls in opposite directions"—vocalized in arguments from the mouths on either
side of his head—the end result of which is the "paradoxical expression of [his] inability to act … within which the poem's present is
defined."[4] But the poem's present, of course, is defined by action.
The present progressive form of the verb "to ride" in the poem's title
conjures the image of a poet in the very act of "Riding Westward."
As Joe Glasser points out, "Donne is not only looking but moving
in the opposite direction" from that which he thinks is correct.[5] The
speaker is capable, then, of acting, but not of acting in the way he
believes he should because his body and the mortal world that sur-
rounds it limit this type of action. Yet the speaker has not actually
accepted "pleasure or business"—or both—as his soul's "first mover"
as he claims to have done in line 9, for this poem is—in and of
itself—an act of devotion, which is for this speaker, as he explains
in line 2, "the intelligence that moves." Instead of Sloane's "curiously
Janus-faced man," I suggest that we find a devoted man, consumed
with thoughts of Christ and the crucifixion. Though, like all mortal
men, this man cannot help but ride westward toward death. This
poem, therefore, as many of Donne's poems, doesn't call for something to happen, but seeks to explain why something is currently
happening. It is diagnostic rather than prescriptive. If the speaker
in "Good Friday" continues riding westward, he will eventually cir-
cumnavigate the globe and wind up back where he started. I will
argue that poem itself, as a formal act, works in precisely the same
way. Its circular reasoning is intended more for the speaker himself—and for his mortal readers—than for the ears of God, no matter that, as William Halewood points out, "God enters [the poem]
to be spoken to."[6] More importantly, because Donne and his readers

---

[3] Ibid., 57.

[4] Ibid., 40–41.

[5] Joe Glasser, "'Goodfriday, 1613': A Soul's Form," *College Literature*
13, no. 2 (1986): 171.

[6] William H. Halewood, "The Predicament of the Westward Rider,"
Studies in Philology 93, no. 2 (1996): 228.

are mortals, unable to hold two thoughts in their heads at the same time, we must perforce reject Sloane's notion of "simultaneously dual directionality," and instead move linearly through the poem from one thought to the next.[7]

There is an order to the poem just as there is an order to salvation. Are we to imagine the speaker riding beneath the banner of John Calvin who, according to R. T. Kendall "insists we cannot truly repent until we are first assured of God's grace" or, instead, beneath the banner of Theodore Beza, "Calvin's successor in Geneva," who "tends to put repentance before faith"?[8] That is to say, can the speaker act on his own behalf and repent, or must he patiently— and passively—await his "turn to God" which necessarily follows his being "given faith."[9] I will insist that Donne's speaker displays a greater affinity for the *ordo salutis* as posited by Beza than Calvin because although the poem is a meditation on his inability to act, the poem itself betokens action. He repents the implicit weakness— the sin—of all mortal men as he rides westward around the curve of the earth toward death where Christ, his potential redeemer, and immortality await the faithful.

If one reads "Good Friday" in conjunction with Donne's "Holy Sonnets," the first glaring difference is the absence in "Good Friday" of the drama so conspicuous at the onset of so many of the sonnets. Instead of demanding an action—of God (Sonnet 1, 14) or the angels (Sonnet 7) or Death (Sonnet 10) or Christ (Sonnet 18)—Donne asks the reader to imagine an analogical idea. The hortatory tone so prevalent in the "Holy Sonnets," gives way to a complex analogy—already anachronistic in its use of the Ptolemaic Universe—through which Donne asks the reader to patiently follow him:

> Let man's soul be a sphere, and then, in this,
> The intelligence that moves, devotion is,

We have the formation "Let ... then" in the first two lines, the language of what Joe Glaser calls a "Euclidian problem" or

---

[7] Sloane, *Donne, Milton, and The End of Humanist Rhetoric*, 60.

[8] R. T. Kendall, *Calvin and English Calvinism to 1649* (Milton Keynes, UK: Paternoster, 1997), 35, 29.

[9] Ibid., 26.

"mathematical proof."[10] Then, in the following two lines, we have a similar formation that builds upon the first—as this happens, so this happens—and so on throughout this section, each subsequent set of two lines building upon the concept previously elaborated:

> And as the other spheres, by being grown
> Subject to foreign motions, lose their own,
> And being by others hurried every day,
> Scarce in a year their natural form obey;
> Pleasure or business, so, our souls admit
> For their first mover, and are whirled by it.

This type of poetry, as J. V. Cunningham observes, is "not merely subject to logical analysis but logical in form," the lines "conceived and expressed syllogistically," the syllogism itself a type of circle, where the reader must return again and again to the primary premise from which the following premises are derived.[11] In the beginning of the poem, Donne abandons the simple commands addressed to God, Christ, and Death precisely because he wants and needs his readers to follow him. Moving from assumption, to elaboration, to further elaboration, he leads the reader along who must patiently keep step to this circular dance. As Sibyl Severance points out, Donne himself defines the movement of the spheres as a dance in lines 25–26 of his "Upon the translation of the Psalmes":

> The Spheres have Musick, but they have no tongue,
> Their harmony is rather danc'd than sung.[12]

In one of the most insightful pieces of scholarship on the circular form of "Good Friday 1613. Riding Westward," Severance argues that its "structure, beyond the shifts and contradictions of the verbal text, marks man's path toward resurrection, reshaping"—as Donne

---

[10] Glaser, "'Goodfriday, 1613': A Soul's Form," 171.

[11] J. V. Cunningham, "Logic and Lyric: Marvell, Dunbar, and Nashe," in *Tradition and Poetic Structure: Essays in Literary History and Criticism* (Denver: Alan Swallow, 1960), 41.

[12] Donne, quoted in Sibyl Lutz Severance, "Soul, Sphere, and Structure in 'Goodfriday, 1613. Riding Westward,'" *Studies in Philology* 84, no. 1 (1987): 28.

himself once said in a sermon—"'this flat map to roundnesse.'"[13] Focusing on sight, Severance evokes the image of Janus when she argues that the "double vision of the Metaphysicals" manifests—in this poem—through the instrument of "double text," a "tenuous balance" lying "between the disparate perceptions granted by word (a mutable appearance) and form (a sustaining reality)."[14] This would seem to contradict Sir Phillip Sidney's insistence in his "Defense of Poesy" that "each word" be weighted by "proportion ... to the dignity of the subject,"[15] that is, that form must match content, and indeed, Severance, wonders how to "reconcile the disorder and contradictions of the journey, recounted by the verbal text, with the ordered serenity set forth by Donne's fair form."[16] The problem Severance has with the content, though, lies in the very nature of life on earth, which is *not* serenely ordered. The author does not lose control of his words, but rather—through them—he decries the "perturbations" and "disunion" of the mortal life of all men.[17]

David Reid asserts that "one of the first things we become aware of in a poem by Donne is the control exerted by thought."[18] He explains that readers "have to follow him if [they] are to make anything of his poetry."[19] Sloane takes this a step further, proposing that the reader not only follows him, but "he becomes someone else," that is, he becomes the poet who wrote the lines.[20] Sloane observes that "there is a certain estrangement in the person we become when we read Donne," an intense "alienation from the object of desire."[21] This makes sense when the object of desire is a devotion to God so profound that it leads to the "best days" of the speaker in Sonnet 19: his tongue paralyzed into silence, his body uncontrollably "shake[ing] with fear" (line 14). Discussing "Good Friday," how-

---

[13] Ibid., 27.

[14] Ibid., 30.

[15] Sidney, "The Defense of Poesy," in *The Norton Anthology of English Literature*, 959.

[16] Severance, "Soul, Sphere, and Structure," 29.

[17] Ibid.

[18] Reid, *The Metaphysical Poets* (Edinburgh Gate, UK: Pearson Education, 2000), 30.

[19] Ibid.

[20] Sloane, *Donne, Milton, and The End of Humanist Rhetoric*, 279.

[21] Ibid., 281.

ever, Sloane argues the obverse of the idea that the reader becomes
the author, insisting instead that Donne becomes the reader of his
own writing. Just as the reader must "follow" the "control exerted by
thought" in order to make anything of the poetry, so Donne must
follow his own line of reasoning in order to gain what he hopes is
salvation, but what he describes as an untenable act of faith.

The long conceit that bridges the gap between the geometry
of the opening lines and the prayer of the closing lines consists of
a series of images that "the speaker [expressly] does *not* see."[22] If
he were looking toward the East, the direction in which his "soul's
form bends," he "should see a Sun by rising, set" (lines 10, 11). The
key word here is "should," and—if we read closely—we see the word
has several connotations. First, the speaker believes that "should" he
turn his eyes eastward toward salvation—a conditional premise—he
would expect to see there an image of Christ on the cross. Second,
the speaker believes that he himself "should" make that turn, it being
an obligation because that motion is the "natural form" of the prime
mover "devotion." But a third possible meaning of this word subverts the first two by implying that although this vision "should" be
there, "And by that setting endless day beget," the image of Christ
on the cross is, paradoxically, conspicuously absent. This reading
echoes the final lines of "Holy Sonnet 7," in which the speaker asks
God to "Teach [him] how to repent; for that's as good / As if thou
hadst sealed my pardon with thy blood" (lines 13–14), the heretical
implication being that Christ has not already sealed the speaker's
pardon with his blood at an earlier juncture in soteriological history. Of course, in "Good Friday," Donne attempts to clear up the
ambiguous possibilities of the word "should" in the lines that follow: "But that Christ on this cross did rise and fall / Sin had eter-
nally benighted all" (lines 13–14). Regardless of Donne's insistence
in these lines that Christ did rise and fall, all three interpretations of
the word "should" in the previous lines insist that neither the reader
nor the speaker sees the image of Christ on the cross.

The justification for this seemingly self-inflicted blindness
appears to come first in lines 15–16 when the speaker halfheartedly
ventures, "Yet dare I almost be glad I do not see / That spectacle,
of too much weight for me." Here, the speaker justifies an action

---

[22] Severance, "Soul, Sphere, and Structure," 31.

that has already happened—his turning toward the West—and one that is currently happening—his riding Westward. "That spectacle" of Christ on the cross is "too much weight" for him to bear, and he is "almost" glad he "do[es] not see" it (lines 16, 15). The poem moves from this point into a further justification, and though the reader might be tempted to equate the series of images as a parallel expression of the circular conceit-building that opens the poem, the images actually serve as a sequence of wholly separate examples that coalesce into a panoramic view of Christ on the cross. Just as Donne exerts control by means of complex thought, argues Reid, so he also exerts control "in the piling up of examples"—a spilling over of *copiae*—which shows his "power of invention" and also "calls attention to the ability of the speaker to keep so much in play without the thought folding up."[23] Every two lines provide a new image, from an implied allusion to Moses hiding between the rocks as God passes over (lines 17–18), to the earthquake and eclipse that occurred at Christ's crucifixion (lines 19–20), to an image of Christ's pierced hands on an enormous cross that spans a Ptolemaic Universe (lines 21–22), to an infinitely high zenith where God sits both above and below us (lines 23–25), to the blood of Christ congealing in our souls and pooling in the dust below the cross (lines 25–27), to God's flesh "ragg'd and torn" in Christ's body (lines 27–28). The pace seems almost frantic in its attempt to justify the rhetorical question implicit in lines 15–16. These are all reasons he dare "almost be glad [he does] not see." They pile up because each, in itself, remains unable to satisfy the speaker's hunt for justification, and we return cyclically to the same original need for the speaker to explain why he currently rides westward. Within this middle section of the poem, then, another circle emerges, a hermeneutic circle where the parts cannot be separated from the whole, nor the whole from the parts, a circle that leads round to the ending of the poem, in which we find the same axiomatic reasoning that opened it, in yet another attempt to explain precisely the same problem: the present moment.

Sloane writes that "to the present, the past brings precedents and the future offers consequences," their juxtaposition suggesting "a lesson in prudent behavior" that must be enacted in the present as

---

[23] Reid, *The Metaphysical Poets*, 31.

"intelligence."[24] Within "Good Friday," the reader identifies Christ's crucifixion as the precedent of the past toward which the speaker's soul bends, a precedent that is "present yet unto [his] memory" (line 34) and manifests itself as the devotion that should be the soul's first mover. The future toward which he rides as a mortal man is, of course, death, but the future beyond death is his concern. He need not be Janus-faced to take account of both, for although the speaker rides toward his inevitable demise, death often sneaks up from behind like "time's winged chariot" and although he "remembers" Christ's crucifixion as an event that happened in the past, Christ— the potential redeemer—awaits mortal man beyond death in the future.

Just as a flat map curled into a circle yields the inevitable meeting of east and west, so the end of the poem curls around to meet the beginning. "I turn my back to thee but to receive / Corrections" (lines 37–38), the persona confesses, providing yet another explanation for why he rides westward. But the proposed listener this time is Christ, and neither the logic of what Barbara Lewalski calls the "preparatory stage," nor the "intellectual analysis of the crucifixion" in the "long central section" will provide an adequate explanation for the speaker's "apparent failure in proper religious devotion."[25] A new answer to the question must be proposed in the "prayer to Christ" that emerges "from the meditative exercise"[26] of the poem in lines 37–42:

> I turn my back to thee but to receive
> Corrections, till thy mercies bid thee leave.
> O think me worth thine anger; punish me;
> Burn off my rusts and my deformity
> Restore thine image so much, by thy grace,
> That thou may'st know me, and I'll turn my face.

Here again, as in the opening eight lines, we see the math-ematical axiom: *let* it be imagined that I have turned my back to

[24] Sloane, *Donne, Milton, and The End of Humanist Rhetoric*, 58.

[25] Barbara Lewalski, "John Donne: Writing After the Copy of a Met-aphorical God," *Protestant Poetics and the Seventeenth-Century Religious Lyric* (Princeton, NJ: Princeton Univ. Press, 1984), 278.

[26] Ibid.

you—Christ—to receive lashings ... *then* "think me worth thine anger" and "punish me," for *if* you restore to me your image ... *then* I will repent and follow you. Superficially, Donne appears to be conducting some type of barter with God: if you do this, then I will do this. But upon further inspection, we see that this blasphemous deal making is instead a plea. The terms of the barter-to-be are out of the speaker's hands and hinge solely on God taking action: I can do this, if—and only if—you first do something for me. "The feebleness of the argument," which in this case lies in the false proposition to perform an act that has already been performed—turning westward—displays, according to Reid, "Donne's helplessness to change his heart as he ought."[27] If we take the "all-or-nothing rhetoric" literally, there is no barter at all: I can't do this, the persona effectively says to Christ on the cross; you must make me do it.

Although this seems to follow the *ordo salutis* as posited by Calvin wherein faith precedes repentance—you must make me do it, you must give me faith—the persona has "drawn [this] conclusion by reflecting upon [him]self," a process anticipated by Beza, and called by William Perkins the "practicall syllogism."[28] If "everyone that believes is the child of God," and the persona is a believer, then he is necessarily "the child of God."[29] We know he is a believer from the lines preceding the conclusion: "thou look'st towards me, / O Savior, as thou hang'st upon the tree" (35–36) These lines leave no room for debate; they are statements of what the speaker believes to be fact. And the following conclusion—which I have already quoted above—ties directly to Beza's belief that "God obliges Himself to act when we come forward with faith."[30] Here again we find the "if ... then" language of geometry. The "biblical banner" for this type of proof lies embedded, according to Kendall in 2 Peter 1:10: "Give diligence to make your calling and election sure: for if ye do these things, ye shall never fall."[31] The speaker in Donne's poem is nothing if not diligent, and diligence is an *act* of the will. When he proposes to "turn his face" in the last line of the poem, the turning becomes an

---

[27] Reid, *The Metaphysical*, 83.
[28] Kendall, *Calvin and English Calvinism*, 8.
[29] Ibid., 9.
[30] Ibid., 35.
[31] Ibid., 9.

act of devotion, the same type of devotion that he describes in the first lines of the poem as the "intelligence that moves" (2). We are right back where we started, and because the speaker still resides in the world of the flesh, his devotion to God will of course be subject to the foreign motions of human pleasure and business, and so on, and so forth. He is "hurried" along through the poem—and through the life of which he writes in the poem—because it is the nature of *tempus* to *fugit* when viewed through a mortal lens. But even as he claims passivity in his elaborately imagined conceit, the very fact that he actively uses his imagination points toward both his own agency and that of his actively engaged reader. As the speaker rides along, he keeps his eyes fixed on the west unfolding before him so that he does not fall from his horse, but he believes his open eyes, in and of themselves, represent their own kind of fall, a subversion of the supernatural by the natural. It is within the devotional and formal *act* of writing the poem—a manifestation of his will—that he repents of the sin inherent in all mortal men, thereby actively seeking the supernatural. The practical syllogism yields an active devotee, but action must be re-iterated. The step-by-step order to salvation leads, inevitably, back to the beginning where a re-view of the present moment leads the disciple toward re-penance.

University of Georgia

"Broken-Backed" Texts: Meritocracy and Misogyny in Ben Jonson's *The Forrest*

Don E. Wayne

> Mediocribus esse poetis
> Non homines, non Dii, non concessere columnae.
> —Horace, *Ars Poetica*, H & S, VIII, 330, lines 389–90

> But neither, Men, nor Gods, nor Pillars meant,
> Poets should ever be indifferent.
> —Ben Jonson, trans., *Horace, of the Art of Poetry*,
> 1640, H & S, VIII, 331, lines 555–56[1]

IN my early years of graduate study, I was told by a professor who liked my work that a paper I had written was interesting, even original, but that it was a "broken-backed essay." Puzzled by the phrase I asked him to explain, and he informed me that I had really attempted to compose two essays and the result was a "broken" piece of literary criticism, something going simultaneously in two directions. Moreover, he pointed out that at times one of these directions seemed to oppose the vector of the other. That made for contradiction, confusion, difficulty in reading. Ultimately, he seemed to say, "what we've got here is a failure to communicate!"—it is perhaps no coincidence that this encounter occurred around the same time as the release of Stuart Rosenberg's film, *Cool Hand Luke*! (1967). But the professor hastened to encourage me because of my "potential" to think and write more coherently and even with some originality. That paper was on *Hamlet*, and it later became a centerpiece of

---

[1] Citations to Jonson are from *Ben Jonson*, ed. C. H. Herford, Percy Simpson, and Evelyn Simpson, 11 vols. (New York: Oxford, 1925–52), hereafter cited in the text as H & S.

an MA thesis I wrote on the topic "Self-Consciousness in Shake-spearean Drama." I doubt that the later version had overcome the disability of the earlier one; probably because by then I had begun to suspect that the professional diagnosis that someone has a writing "problem," because they have difficulty accepting accepted rhetorical protocols, was itself the problem. But when I was told of my "problem" in my first year of graduate school, I probably did work to remedy it with the effect that my writing no doubt became more clear and distinct, but also more cramped and conventional, qualities that then required learning to unlearn, "Broken-backed" is a phrase that has stayed with me my entire academic and professional life, and I think I've only recently begun to effectively grasp the significance of a metaphor that conventionally signifies a communication "problem" or even "failure," for what I consider to be a needed shift in our thinking about thinking, and in our thinking about writing.

They Confound Knowledge with Knowledge

That paper on Hamlet and the MA thesis that developed out of it reflected the influence of a number of books and articles on Shakespeare that dealt with epistemological and ontological questions, including Anne Righter (Barton), *Shakespeare and the Idea of the Play* (1962), and Robert Ornstein, *The Moral Vision of Jacobean Tragedy* (1960).[2] Righter-Barton's book interested me because of its focus on metadrama, a kind of reflexivity of form and content. And one passage in Ornstein particularly intrigued me:

> . . . [T]he crisis which Jacobean tragedy reflects is epistemological, not moral or ideological. The dramatists are not torn between humanistic and antihumanistic views of man. They are caught between old and new ways of determining the realities upon which moral values rest. In an age of rapid intellectual and cultural change, they—and not they alone—confound knowledge with knowledge.

---

[2] Anne Righter (Barton), *Shakespeare and the Idea of the Play* (London: Chatto and Windus, 1962); Robert Ornstein, *The Moral Vision of Jacobean Tragedy* (Madison: Univ. of Wisconsin Press, 1960), 6.

The last phrase, "confound knowledge with knowledge," is taken from the philosophical, though villainous, Flamineo's dying speech in John Webster's play *The White Devil* (1612). Ornstein's reference may seem out of place in a statement purporting to generalize the fundamental "crisis" confronted by the Jacobean dramatists. Yet while the character of Flamineo is sometimes described as overshadowing in magnitude the play's title character, his sister Vittoria Corombona, it is, I would argue, Vittoria, "the white devil," who raises the most important epistemological, legal, political, and ultimately moral questions in the play, and who strategically confounds knowledge with knowledge by means of her eloquent speech to the court demanding that the proceedings be carried out in the vernacular rather than Latin so that the general populace can understand what is going on.[3] By 1974, only a few years later, I taught a course in which the readings included both *The White Devil* and George Jackson's letters in *Soledad Brother.*[4] I was able to correlate in an ironic yet consistent way Vittoria's defiance of an Italian Renaissance court with the situation of Angela Davis's trial, since the continuities on the basis of gender and the social and cultural struggle for women's rights and for the principle of judiciary transparency were counterweights to the historical discontinuity in terms of race and class.

Ornstein's claim that "the crisis which Jacobean tragedy reflects is epistemological" caught my attention because it fit with my sense of Hamlet's dilemma and with my sense of what was most interesting about Jacobean drama (and not just tragedy). And I suppose the question of epistemology also seemed more fundamental to me for my own time than that of the moral or the ideological (in Ornstein's sense of that term). One qualification, however: Ornstein's use of "ideological" involves a more limited semantic reference than my understanding of it; that is, his use of the term involves something like a conscious political doctrine or political orientation, as is still largely the case today in conventional usage by politicians,

---

[3] John Webster, *The White Devil*, ed. Clive Hart, Fountainwell Drama Texts 16 (Edinburgh: Oliver and Boyd; Berkeley: Univ. of California Press, 1970), III, ii, lines 9–360, 49–58.

[4] George Jackson, *Soledad Brother: The Prison Letters of George Jackson* (New York: Coward-McCann, 1970).

journalists, and some historians and political theorists, whereas I think I already had a notion of ideology as something largely unconscious. Even at the start of graduate school, I believe I was intuitively aware of how ideology is manifested, among other ways, through socialization in both the epistemological and the behavioral norms of a discipline or a profession. I think it was not accidental that studies like Ornstein's appeared in the 1960s, a time of cultural crisis when changing social mores generated by the civil rights movement, the revival of feminist activism, and the anti-war movement challenged received foundations of knowledge. In this regard, what may have seemed gratuitous in my earlier allusion to the phrase "failure to communicate" in *Cool Hand Luke* can be seen to have had broad social and cultural resonance in that specific historical conjuncture. I think something similar may be happening today, or needs to happen. Because, despite the innovations of the past half-century, there have been residual forms of epistemological constraint that have inhibited innovation and adaptation to new social, cultural, and ecological conditions.

I'm working on a book now that is another "broken-backed" project, and probably one characterized by more than one break, that is, a mode of analysis and interpretation that involves multiple and sometimes contradictory lines of reasoning, partly by design in order to get away from the very notion of a "line" of reasoning. Readers who may know of my earlier work will be aware that I have written extensively on Ben Jonson. My current project has brought me back to Jonson after twenty years of having left that particular field of study. Yet as I write, I'm driven by conflicting, even contradictory vectors of thinking about the status not only of Jonson studies, but of the humanities and social sciences more generally. In the past I wrote on Jonson in a manner that attempted to engage with the texts of an author who occupies a major yet eccentric position in the English literary canon while also relating those texts to contexts that may have been largely ignored or misunderstood by most previous literary critics. That sounds like an arrogant assertion. But I believe it comes out of a response developed over many years to what I consider a disciplinary arrogance that has hindered innovative scholarship in the social sciences and humanities. There are of course notable exceptions to the claim I make here, and I have tried to acknowledge many of these exceptions in this book project.

If one looks at the history of the natural sciences over the past sixty years one finds extensive theoretical and experimental research developed across disciplines, leading to the foundation of new disciplines such as neuroscience, biochemistry, bioengineering, computer science, etc. In the humanities and social sciences, by contrast, even efforts at bringing together disciplines tend to be focused on models of interdisciplinarity, the prefix "inter" suggesting a rather nervous apprehension of a possible loss of disciplinary integrity and authority. "Inter" is a sort of relational term, but it suggests a relation between two or more distinct entities. I submit that part of the problem with our thinking in disciplinary terms is that it is itself a manifestation of a problem that the notion of "interdisciplinary" is straining to overcome: most disciplines in the humanities and the social sciences have continued for generations to be founded on an epistemology that focuses on energy-entity relationships, involving efficient causality among data understood as substantive, discrete facts or concepts; in other words, a kind of substantialism in which the concepts through which we communicate are themselves conceived as entities. This is one reason why binary thinking persists even among proponents of one or another strain of "poststructuralism." The alternative to such an epistemology is one that conceptualizes relationships in a more complex way, as relations between and among relations. This in turn means thinking of *thinking* itself as more complex than in terms of a singular kind of logic in which relations among terms are strictly analytic, linear, causal, and governed exclusively by the principle of non-contradiction. Such thinking has a function in certain stages of research, in science and in other fields. But so does another kind of thinking which has been practiced in several forms in the past but is sorely lacking in the dominant discipline-based thinking of today: I'm referring to dialectical thinking.

Structural Irony: Plato and Aristotle

I've always wondered about one of the meanings of mimesis or "imitation" in Plato, that is, in book 3 of *The Republic*, where in discussing Homeric epic poetry Socrates draws the distinction between narration and imitation as two aspects of epic narration in a broader sense, and then asks: "But when the poet speaks in the person of another, may we not say that he assimilates his style to that of the person who, as he informs you, is going to speak?"[5] Socrates then goes on to develop his interrogation of poetic language by delineating three modes, simple narration, imitation (exemplified by the drama, tragedy and comedy), and a hybrid of the two. Ultimately, on the basis of a principle of singular identity, "by the rule already laid down that one man can only do one thing well, and not many; and that one who grasps at many will altogether fail of gaining much reputation in any," he asks "And this is equally true of imitation: no one man can imitate many things as well as he would imitate a single one?" And the dialogue continues to develop the idea of distrust of imitation, or of assimilating the style of others, casting it as a form of deception that is a danger to the state. But then of course, what we are reading is a "dialogue," that is a poetic genre. Aristotle seems to have understood what many later philosophers did not; i.e., that in arguing in behalf of philosophy, Plato wrote as a poet, and as a poet whose principle mode was what Socrates calls "imitation" or a "hybrid" of imitation and narration. Yet it seems that even in our own time commentary on Plato's writings treats Socrates ideas as Plato's, or to put it another way, most commentary takes the Platonic philosophy to be what the commentator can extract as ideas, or moral values, from what is said by Socrates, or rather from what is *asked* by Socrates and what, through dialogue, Socrates induces his interlocutors to say. So if the stated philosophy and morality of *Republic* 3 is that all imitation is deception, and if that statement is made by the medium of an author who "assimilates" the style of the main character in the dialogue, does that make the author's rhetorical strategy a "deception," or are we to recognize that the main character may be portrayed as the deceiver, an unreliable source for our acceptance of the concluding statements his interlocutors arrive at as "truth?" My question is an elaboration of something Harry Berger, Jr., has recognized and described as the "structural irony" of Plato's

---

[5] Quotations from Plato's *Republic* are from *The Dialogues of Plato,* trans. Benjamin Jowett, 4th ed. (Oxford: Clarendon Press, 1953).

presentation, as distinct from the more conventionally understood "Socratic irony" of the subject he represents.[6]

Structural Irony:
More's *Utopia* and Sidney's *Defence*

Two millennia later Thomas More understood this aspect of Plato's dialogues when he wrote book 1 of his *Utopia* (a frame dialogue written in reverse chronological order after having composed the monologue of book 2). But More is famous for having given signs of his ironic intention in the philological word games of names and phrases he played, and in the way he related the two books of his larger work.[7] More's text is in a sense a humanist manual on how to read carefully and critically. And it is interesting that in one of the first works of poetics in English, Sir Philip Sidney's *The Defence of Poesy*, begun as early as ca. 1579 but published posthumously in 1595, there is a reference to More's *Utopia* that appears to show that Sidney missed the game and the lesson of More's text. I will explain what I mean by "appears to show" in a moment. Sidney uses this reference to *Utopia* and to More as an illustration of his point that the poet surpasses the philosopher's "precepts" and the historian's focus on "the particular truth of things," because the poet provides "a perfect picture" of things, depicting by means of "feigning" both the "general notion" and the "particular example." Sidney's illustrations begin with the feigning of virtuous character traits embodied in heroic individuals depicted in literary works; but he adds the example of the depiction of "a whole commonwealth; as the way of

---

[6] Harry Berger, Jr., *Situated Utterances: Texts, Bodies, and Cultural Representations*; (New York: Fordham Univ. Press, 2005), 50.

[7] The most detailed and revealing analysis of the formal structure and word play in More's *Utopia* is Louis Marin's in his *Utopiques: jeux d'espaces* (Paris: Minuit, 1973). See also Fredric Jameson, "Of Islands and Trenches: Neutralization and the Production of Utopian Discourse," *Diacritics* 7, no. 2 (Summer 1977): 2–21. Jameson's influential linkage of the themes and forms of "utopian dimension" and "national allegory" is refined and amplified most recently in his *Allegory and Ideology* (London, New York: Verso, 2019), 187–215 and passim.

Sir Thomas More's *Utopia*; I say the way, because where Sir Thomas
More erred, it was the fault of the man and not of the poet, for
that way of patterning a commonwealth was most absolute, though
he perchance hath not so absolutely performed it."[8] Sidney is here
missing the point, or *appears* to be missing the point of More's text,
which is that its message is in its form and not in the "absolute" representation of a commonwealth. But so many commentators after
Sidney have made a similar error as readers, some even going so
far as to quote the ideas expressed by "Thomas More" the character in book 1 as necessarily those of Thomas More the author. In
other places Sidney shows himself to be a careful reader, but here
his apparent misunderstanding of More's text is probably a residual effect of two factors: 1) his Protestant bias against More "the
man" who had become a Catholic martyr; and 2), the fact that in the
Defence Sidney deliberately misreads Plato's *Ion* and other dialogues
in order to twist Plato into a defender of the high moral function
Sidney wants to claim for poetry.

Now, to explain why I say Sidney "appears" to miss More's
point. Until recently I had written confidently that Sidney missed
the fundamental poetic point of More's book. But then I read an
essay by Martin Raitiere that surprised, even startled me with its
method combining rhetorical, grammatical, and logical analysis and
exegesis within an interpretive framework that I would describe as
dialectical.[9] Raitiere's essay appeared in 1981, a time when high
theory in literary studies was gaining momentum—feminist criticism, deconstruction, new historicism, and critical methods linked
to the writings of Freud and Marx. On the surface, his approach
was more traditional, but because of his background in comparative literature, his method of stylistic, rhetorical, and philological
analysis was different from what English departments taught their
graduate students. At the same time, Raitiere's perception of dis-
junctions and deformations in Sidney's writing, and his argument
that these elements were deliberate and functional in lending coher-

---

[8] Sir Philip Sidney, *A Defence of Poetry*, in *Miscellaneous Prose of Sir
Philip Sidney*, ed. Katherine Duncan-Jones and Jan van Dorsten (Oxford:
Clarendon Pres, 1973), 86.

[9] Martin N. Raitiere, "The Unity of Sidney's *Apology for Poetry*," *Studies in English Literature* 21, no. 1 (Winter 1981): 37–57.

ence to Sidney's thesis as a whole, placed his work closer to some of
the theoretical criticism of that period. The result is one of the more
complex and persuasive close readings of Sidney's text that we have.

Raitiere acknowledges another influential earlier interpretation
of the *Apology*, that of O. B. Hardison, who claimed Sidney's text
was a kind of broken-backed composition, probably the result of
an earlier first part and a later revision of only the second part, that
Hardison saw as reflecting a fundamental change in Sidney's aesthetic. In summarizing Hardison's view, Raitiere writes: "The work
as we have it remains an unstable amalgam of 'two voices,' the earlier
one 'humanistic in the manner of Boccaccio, Politian, and Tasso' and
the later one 'neo-classic in the manner of Scaliger, Castelvetro, and
Ben Jonson.' Thus the problem of the *Apology for Poetry*: an inconsistency in argument, even a fundamental contradiction, between
one part of the work and another." Raitiere admits that Hardison's
observation of this inconsistency has empirical validity, but he goes
on to dispute the conclusion Hardison draws from his observation.
For Raitiere, the "inconsistency" is part of a larger strategy that gives
the work a "genuine synthetic unity of its own" (39). I find Raitiere's emphasis on "unity" here and in his title a little puzzling, even
misleading, in that it suggests the orthodoxy of the New Criticism
(as exemplified in two famous titles from that movement, Cleanth
Brooks's *The Well Wrought Urn* and W. K. Wimsatt's *The Verbal
Icon*). Those images suggest a unity that is relatively static, and what
I find especially interesting and persuasive in Raitiere's analysis and
argument is that whatever "unity" he discovers through his reading is, rather, something dynamic, an instance in prose of the poetic
quality Sidney refers to in his argument as *energeia* (as distinct from
the related term *enargeia*), an ancient term developed with multiple connotations in Renaissance poetic theory, for a content-driven
vital aspect of poetry that Sidney translates as "forcibleness."[10]
This dynamic aspect of Sidney's writing is further evident in Rai-

---

[10] For Sidney's use of the term and his possible indebtedness to both
Tasso's and Scaliger's divergent concepts of *energeia*, see Annabel M. Pat-
terson, *Hermogenes and the Renaissance: Seven Ideas of Style* (Princeton, NJ:
Princeton Univ. Press, 1970), 131–33. George Puttenham in *The Art of
English Poesie (1589): A Critical Edition*, ed. Frank Whigham and Wayne
A. Rebhorn (Ithaca, NY: Cornell Univ. Press, 2007), names both terms,

tiere's elaboration on antinomies and contradictions in the *Apology* (even at the level of a single sentence where, for example, in the section where Sidney compares the philosopher and the poet, Raitiere identifies a "syntactic hierarchy . . . [in which] the philosopher (main clause) governs or outranks the poet (two dependent clauses away), although this is precisely the opposite of what Sidney set out to prove" (42–43). Raitiere also discusses how in a section in which "Sidney's general theme . . . is reconciliation or mediation (of abstract and concrete, by the poet)," the passage in question, "seems rather to testify to failed mediation or disjunction . . ." (47). "Failed mediation," and "refused mediation" are terms repeated in this analysis, and ultimately Raitiere suggests that the fundamental differences, inconsistencies, or contradictions between the first portion of the *Apology*, the "oration," and the second, the "digression," are not as Hardison argued an effect of later interpolation, but are rather by design: "Hardison has, if anything, only underestimated the true extent of Sidney's duplicitous voice" (53). So it is especially interesting that Raitiere's notion of the text's "unity" depends on terms such as "failed," "refused," "disjunction," "duplicitous." I haven't done justice to the intricacy, precision, and persuasive force of Raitiere's reading, but I would say that rather than an instance of New Critical "Unity" it seems more like a variant of deconstruction, not in the mode associated with Jacques Derrida, but perhaps that of Stanley Fish. Not surprisingly, Raitiere cites as a source for his thinking about Sidney's *Apology* Fish's early book *Self-Consuming Artifacts*, which Raitiere glosses as being "about the kind of poetry and prose that works by disappointing or consuming its own ostensible rules and the complacent reader's expectations"[11] (43n). There may also be one more contradictory element in what Raitiere has uncovered through his elegant and rigorous reading of Sidney. That arises from the odd conclusion he draws, based on his idea of Sidney's theme of "failed mediation" between subject and object, or "a contradictory or anisomorphic relation between content and structure," that hence, there is "a problem or irony that conditions our work at all points.

---

providing more elaborate definitions of each than Sidney; see book 3 ch. 3, 227 and eds. footnote.

[11] Stanley Fish, *Self-Consuming Artifacts* (Berkeley: Univ. of California Press, 1972).

Its medium is *never* its message" (53). Yet if Hardison, and those following his lead in holding to the analytic logic of non-contradiction, viewed the structure as broken and needing fixing, which Hardison proposed Sidney might have done had he not died at an early age, and if Raitiere has demonstrated to the contrary that the structure is deliberately broken, then how is this not also a demonstration that the message of Sidney's *Apology* is, indeed, in a very fundamental respect, that the medium *is* the message?

Raitiere's interpretation of the *Apology*, or, as I have been referring to it, the *Defence*, has had the effect of changing my thinking about Sidney's reference to Thomas More. I was inclined to view Sidney, who is often a careful and conscientious reader, as having suffered a lapse in judgment and become a "complacent reader" of More's *Utopia*. But I have now changed what I wrote previously to say that Sidney "appears to misread" *Utopia*, in a manner similar to his deliberate and tactical misreading of Plato's *Ion*. One might even view these "misreadings" as devices or cues to a discerning and knowledgeable reader. Returning for a moment to the Platonic dialogues, it is important to acknowledge that if Plato gives any signs to the reader of "structural irony," as distinct from what is conventionally referred to by the phrase "Socratic irony," they are not as obvious as those reading cues employed by More in *Utopia* or by Sidney in the *Defence*, which is one reason Plato continues to be read as a philosopher more commonly than as a poet.

Having learned from Raitiere that Sidney is himself a writer engaged in a serious game of "structural irony," I now think Sidney's misreadings are by design and I now view his *Defence* as strategically structured like More's, with two sections that are deliberately inconsistent and contradictory; and I now believe the meaning of both texts lies in their formal strategies, governed by the cultural and social restraints of their respective times, for training critical, independent, and imaginative readers. Sidney's theoretical defense of poetry can be thought of as fitting the genre More named in the title of his book, a kind of utopian literature in both its form and its meaning, and I would argue that the same can be said of other ostensibly philosophical writings characterized by structural irony, including the Platonic dialogues that touch on poetry and poetics, and the two parts of Kant's aesthetic with its dialectic between the "Analytic of the Beautiful" and the "Analytic of the Sublime." The kind of "spatial play" that Louis Marin designated as a fundamental motif of utopian discourse, that he analyzed in such careful detail along with his notion of such discourse as an "ideological critique of ideology" is I think a facet of most fiction, not just that specifically categorized under the genre of utopia. And while Marin distinguishes this fictive form of "critique" from conceptual forms in philosophical discourse, I'd suggest that there are fictive aspects of the latter and especially in philosophical discourse on aesthetics, such as Sidney's and Kant's, that entail a similar capacity for what Marin means by the phrase "ideological critique of ideology."[12]

We have no specific evidence of how Jonson read More's *Utopia*. He includes More in a celebratory list of England's principal scholars and writers (*H&S, Timber, or Discoveries,* 8.591); and there is an extant volume from Jonson's library with his signature and annotations, containing More's *History of Richard III* (1566), and some of More's poems.[13] It would be interesting to have a sense of how Jonson interpreted More's rhetoric in *Utopia.* I would speculate that he would have grasped the aspect of More's writing that Sidney rhetorically represented himself as missing, if only because in his own practice as a poet Jonson employs the device of structural irony, as I have argued previously in relation to other Jonsonian texts, and as I hope to demonstrate in an extended reading of *The Forrest,* of which this essay gives a preliminary view.

I have written previously about *The Forrest* with somewhat different emphasis on Jonson's relation to Sidney where I began by referring to another groundbreaking study of Sidney's *Defence,* Margaret Ferguson's *Trials of Desire.*[14] Ferguson points to the blindness of modern criticism in failing to recognize that Sidney's text was political as much as it was poetical. She writes: "It is an irony of literary history that those who rely on Kant, Aristotle,

---

[12] Louis Marin, "Theses on Ideology and Utopia," trans. Fredric Jameson, *Minnesota Review,* N.S., 6 (Spring 1976): 71–75.

[13] Center for Thomas More Studies, https://www.thomasmorestudies. org/library.html.

[14] Don E. Wayne, "Jonson's Sidney: Legacy and Legitimation in *The Forrest,* in *Sir Philip Sidney's Achievements,* ed. M. J. B. Allen, Dominic Baker-Smith, Arthur F. Kinney, and Margaret M. Sullivan (New York: AMS Press, 1990), 227–50.

or other theories of aesthetic formalism to fence off a sphere for innocent art (and innocent criticism) simply repeat a defensive strategy which Sidney himself employs in a dialectical and self-reflexive way."[15]

Ferguson, in an earlier version of her study, had argued that Sidney's defense of poetry "is also a defense of the speaking subject."[16] That she dropped this assertion in her final version implies a more scrupulous historicizing of Sidney's text, an acknowledgment that ultimately, for Sidney the speaking subject was aristocratic and masculine. It would of course remain masculine for some time to come. But already in the next generation, poetry and its defense would provide the basis for a model of the speaking subject as independent of a hierarchy determined by signs of blood. Ben Jonson takes up Sidney's defense of the speaking subject along with the neoclassical strains of the *Defence* as part of a strategy for legitimating power along meritocratic if not democratic lines.[17] In so doing, he is both identifying with Sidney's authority and struggling with it. Within fifteen years of Sidney's death, in a poem addressed to Sidney's daughter Elizabeth, Jonson appropriates the aristocratic legend and lays claim to sharing in Sidney's apotheosis by identifying the "high and noble matter" of his own verse with those "moods which the god-like Sidney oft did prove" (*For.* 12, lines 89–91). Yet a few lines earlier, Jonson has declared the novelty and originality in form of his own "strange poems," and announced his divergence from Sidneyan models:[18]

---

[15] Ferguson, Margaret W. "Sidney's A Defence of Poetry: A Retrial." *Boundary 2* 7, no. 2 (1979): 63.

[16] Margaret W. Ferguson, *Trials of Desire: Renaissance Defenses of Poetry* (New Haven, CT: Yale Univ. Press, 1983), 140; and "Sidney's A Defence of Poetry: A Retrial," *Boundary 2* 7, no. 2 (1979): 62; M. J. Doherty, *The Mistress Knowledge: Sir Philip Sidney's Defence of Poesie and Literary Architectonics in the English Renaissance* (Nashville: Vanderbilt Univ. Press, 1991).

[17] On Jonson's troubled relationship with the system of courtly patronage and its particular "merit calculus," see Stanley Fish, "Authors-Readers: Jonson's Community of the Same," *Representations* 7 (1984): 26–58. Also see Robert C. Evans, *Ben Jonson and the Poetics of Patronage* (Lewisburg: Bucknell Univ. Press; London: Associated Univ. Presses, 1989).

[18] George Parfitt, "The 'Strangeness' of Ben Jonson's *The Forest*," *Leeds Studies in English*, n.s. 18 (1987): 45–54, has discussed several reasons why

Then all, that have but done my Muse least grace,
　　Shall thronging come, and boast the happy place
They hold in my strange poems, which, as yet,
　　Had not their forme touch'd by an English wit.
　　　　　　　　　　　　　(*For.* 12, lines 79–82)

Focusing on this poem as part of his comprehensive and discriminating study of Jonson's epideictic poetry, Richard Peterson has analyzed the combination of classical allusion and contemporary occasional reference through which Jonson lays claim to the poet's power to animate or "move" his patrons and readers to embody or "stand" for ethical imperatives.[19] Peterson also acknowledges textual evidence of Jonson's representation of discrepancies between the ideal and the actual in the standing of his patrons, though his acknowledgment is attenuated, and I would place greater emphasis on the significance of such discrepancies.[20] By 1616, when this poem is collected in *The Forrest*, Jonson has elaborated his appropriation of the name Sidney into an ideology in which his own identity as an intellectual is secured by the power claimed for poetry in authorizing and legitimating the social order that the poet must serve.

There is, however, more to *The Forrest* than just a textual strategy of self-fashioning. While my reading focuses on social determinants of a psychological struggle for identity and power in this text, it also elaborates on a thesis concerning the history of domesticity

Jonson's poems collected in *The Forrest* might have seemed "strange" to readers of the 1616 folio, and relates these qualities in Jonson's poetry to the religious and political conflicts of the period. He also shares my view that there is a "dialectical" relation between the "old" and the "new" in *The Forrest* (49).

[19] Richard S. Peterson, *Imitation and Praise in the Poems of Ben Jonson* (New Haven, CT: Yale Univ. Press, 1981), 95–99.

[20] Peterson points to Horace's influence on Jonson's way of giving praise, "which involves clear judgment as well as affection and characteristically admits some discrepancy with fact without being merely ironic or satiric" (176). I would add, however, that there are places where the lines between epideictic and satire are blurred by Jonson, particularly in his *Epigrammes*, for which see Don E. Wayne, "Poetry and Power in Ben Jonson's *Epigrammes*: The Naming of 'Facts' or the Figuring of Social Relations?" *Renaissance and Modern Studies* 23 (1979): 79–103.

and the interrelationship of class and gender relations, set forth in my earlier work on Jonson, the Sidneys, and Penshurst.[21] In more recent criticism there has been acknowledgment of the theme of a community based on intellectual merit in Jonson's writings, especially by Ian Donaldson in his very fine biography.[22] But as regards *The Forrest* there has been surprisingly little consideration of another *leitmotif* in this ordered collection of poems, the strains of misogyny that Jonson plays and that he pays as the price of his otherwise valiant call for reform—in a time when status marked by birth and rank was still a strong basis of social hierarchy, and in a time of impending conflict and crisis. Identity for Jonson takes the form of a patriarchal humanism in which meritocracy depends on misogyny, even where aristocratic feminine agency is acknowledged and celebrated.

Jonson's *The Forrest* and the Author Function

Like the *Epigrammes*, *The Forrest* is a collection that Jonson himself edited for the 1616 folio.[23] We are therefore on firm ground in presuming that the structure of the entire sequence of poems is governed by a deliberate design. In offering my interpretation of that organizational scheme I shall not attempt to provide a sequential reading of the entire collection of fifteen poems, for two reasons: First, if *The Forrest* is as complex a text as I believe it to be, then any attempt to treat each poem individually within the scope of a single essay will hardly do justice to that complexity. Second, a linear, poem-by-poem approach is likely to sustain the notion of what T. S.

---

[21] Don E. Wayne, *Penshurst: The Semiotics of Place and the Poetics of History* (Madison: Univ. of Wisconsin Press, 1984).

[22] Ian Donaldson, *Ben Jonson: A Life* (Oxford: Oxford Univ. Press, 2011), 70–71.

[23] One of Colin Burrow's first points in his excellent textual essay on Jonson's poems for the *Cambridge Edition of the Works of Ben Jonson* is to establish that the texts of *Epigrammes* and *The Forrest* are reliably as Jonson ordered them in overseeing production of the 1616 folio: http://universitypublishingonline.org/cambridge/benjonson/k/essays/ The_Poems_textual_essay/1/

Eliot described, I think mistakenly, as Jonson's "poetry of the surface," by connecting the elements of the sequence, horizontally as it
were, without paying sufficient attention to the vertical or paradig-
matic structure, which is determined by a rhetoric that cuts across
the immediately perceptible sequential order.

Alastair Fowler and Jonathan Z. Kamholtz have offered arguments for *The Forrest's* integrated structure.[24] Both studies, while
informative, are limited by the authors' adherence to a linear, thematic approach that takes at face value the rhetoric of the plain style
and the putative Stoic or Christian ethic it displays. Such readings,
driven by assumptions of ethical and thematic coherence, tend to
stabilize what is otherwise an uneasy integration of often contradictory factors determining locutionary strategy and poetic structure. In these poems, as in much of Renaissance literature, the poet's
identity is mediated by his relations with those who possess the
power to authorize his words: his patrons, in Jonson's case mainly,
aside from the king and court, the Sidney family. But in *The Forrest* the poet-patron relationship is complicated to an immeasurable
degree by the fact that a member of the family, Sir Philip Sidney,
was himself a poet; a poet, moreover, who had acquired posthumously what Richard Helgerson describes as symbolic if not official
"laureate" status by the time Jonson was writing.[25] The figure and
the poetic voice of Philip Sidney is central to Jonson's construction
of his own subjectivity in these poems and elsewhere in his work.

I would go so far as to suggest that Jonson understood this
principle by following Sidney's example in becoming a literary the-
orist as much as a poet, by attempting to consecrate his own texts
as "Works" in 1616, and in 1623 by playing a major role in the con-
secration of William Shakespeare through his authorship of the
principal dedicatory poem to the Shakespeare folio. One wonders if
Jonson, who previously had a supervisory relation to the printer of

---

[24] Alastair Fowler, "The Silva Tradition in Jonson's *The Forrest*," in
Poetic Traditions of the English Renaissance, ed. Maynard Mack and George
de Forest Lord (New Haven, CT: Yale Univ. Press, 1982), 163–80; and
Jonathan Z. Kamholtz, "Ben Jonson's Green World: Structure and Imaginative Unity in *The Forrest*," *Studies in Philology* 78, no. 2 (1981): 170–93.

[25] Richard Helgerson, *Self-Crowned Laureates: Spenser, Jonson, Milton
and the Literary System* (Berkeley: Univ. of California Press, 1983), 104.

his own folio, might have also had a role in directing a compositor to use upper-case and an enlarged font for "AUTHOR" in the title of his encomium for the Shakespeare folio:

> To the memory of my beloved,
> The AUTHOR
> Mr. William Shakespeare:
> And
> what he hath left us.[26]

I shall argue here that Jonson appropriates Sidney's poetic authority as well as Bacon's epistemological authority as part of a politics that is ultimately antithetical to the court society of which these aristocrats were members and which Jonson had to serve. That politics emphasizes merit over birth and entails an emergent capitalist ideology concerning the patriarchal family, domestic management, and the work ethic with its hierarchical division of mental and manual labor, as elemental and universal components of the social contract essential to the well-being of the entire commonwealth. Within that framework, Jonson may have been willing to accord some aristocratic women a place on the intellectual side of the division of labor, but the motives of his deference in this regard are ambiguous and the effect of his acknowledgment is, at best, condescending. These, I claim, are the primary factors governing the disposition of the poems in the sequence of *The Forrest* as a whole.

Forrest 4–11: Meritocracy and Misogyny

Since this is a preview of a much longer study of the entire sequence of fifteen poems that forms a chapter of a book in progress, I shall concentrate here, in brief, on some poems at the center of *The Forrest*'s overall structure, poems 4–11. Despite the variety of genres represented in this middle section, a striking feature that most of these poems have in common is the preponderant thematic and figurative concern with women, who are treated in attitudes ranging from condescension to debasement. George Parfitt is one of the earliest

---

[26] *The First Folio of Shakespeare*, ed. Charlton Hinman (New York: W. W. Norton, 1968), 9.

(1969) critics to acknowledge the element of misogyny in Jonson's poetry, when, in describing Jonson's ethics, he concludes "Finally, women in Jonson's poetry are viewed with a mixture of rough abuse and strong admiration."[27] Another early acknowledgment of Jonson's misogyny was Peter Womack's (1986). In what is still, thirty years after its appearance, one of the best studies of Jonson's work for the theater, Womack discusses how "classical culture . . . is a contradictory sign, on the one hand representing a universal humanism, but on the other constituting male difference." And although his book focuses primarily on the drama, Womack quotes here from *Forrest* 7, "'That Women Are but Men's Shadows,'" and comments: "The logic is that men could fully realize themselves only in a world where women didn't exist. But that ideal is gracefully invalidated by the metaphor of the shadow, which draws attention to the inseparability of the sexes. Masculinity is a differential concept: that is, the concept of femininity is necessary to it and remains a part of it, perpetually subverting its attempts to represent its distinctive values as autonomous and universal."[28] While most discussions of Jonson's misogyny have focused on the dramatic works, an important exception is Ann Baynes Coiro's brief yet nuanced comparative study of Aemilia Lanyer and Jonson, to which I shall return below.[29]

In one place, Jonson even employs a rather brutal version of a trope that occurs in Renaissance art manuals, notably, Alberti's *On Painting* (1435), with its governing principles of *ratio* and *virtù*. Alberti advises the (presumably masculine) Florentine painter or sculptor how to realize the neoplatonic ideal of a feminine body. Since in nature all desirable features "were not to be discovered in one body alone," the goal, following the example of the ancient painter Zeuxis, is a rationalized synthesis of the most beautiful examples of different female body parts observable in the city.[30] In

---

[27] G. A. E. Parfitt, "Ethical Thought and Ben Jonson's Poetry," *Studies in English Literature, 1500–1900* 9, no. 11 (Winter 1969): 127.

[28] Peter Womack, *Ben Jonson* (New York: B. Blackwell, 1986), 122–24.

[29] Ann Baynes Coiro, "Writing in Service: Sexual Politics and Class Position in the Poetry of Aemilia Lanyer and Ben Jonson," *Criticism* 35, no. 3 (Summer 1993): 357–76.

[30] Leon Battista Alberti, *On Painting*, trans. Cecil Grayson (New York: Penguin, 1991), 91; see also Ellen Adams, "Fragmentation and the

Forrest 10, Jonson imagines such a synthesis in a rhetorical trope of female figures "crushed into one forme" (line 26). In their prefatory discussion of the text of *The Forrest*, Herford and Simpson seemed at a loss to explain why this poem was included in the collection. They responded to it with an attitude bordering on disgust, asking why Jonson "rewrote it [from an earlier printed version] in so incongruous a form," disdaining it as "ribald," implying that Jonson was himself somewhat embarrassed as they wondered why he included it "without even the clue of a heading," and judging that "it clashes with the whole tone of *The Forrest*."[31] But, given their own acknowledgment that Jonson oversaw the selection and ordering of the poems in *The Forrest*, their assessment strikes me as unjustified and inconsistent with Jonson's own judgment.

If a major theme in *The Forrest* is the correlation of virtuous love and the love of virtue, then it is made in the form of a masculinist and heteronormative version of virtue. Classical female deities are represented in *Forrest* 10 as not to be invoked because they lack correct feminine qualities suitable to a virtuous masculine poetry. The poet refuses to "call on" Pallas while calling her "mankind maid," and Venus is told derisively "Or with thy tribade trine invent new sports; / Thou nor thy looseness with my making sorts." Valerie Traub has identified a homophobic motif in this poem, suggesting that "Jonson's rejection of their 'new sports' implies that tribadism is an illicit form of contact that generates unacceptable forms of literary production."[32] In the poem's closing lines Jonson climaxes his rejection of a catalogue of possible classical mythological sources for poetic inspiration with the following reference to the muses, who are also finally rejected to make way for his own independent, masculine thought on virtuous love:

> Nor all the ladies of the Thespian lake,
> (Though they were crushed into one forme) could make
> A beautie of that merit, that should take my

Body's Boundaries: Reassessing the Body Parts," in *Ancient Anatomical Votives Past, Present, and Future*, ed. Jane Draycott (London: Routledge, 2017), 193–213.

[31] *Ben Jonson*, ed. Herford, Simpson, and Simpson, 8:9–10.

[32] Valerie Traub, *The Renaissance of Lesbianism in Early Modern England* (Cambridge: Cambridge Univ. Press, 2002), 25.

Muse up by commission: No I bring
My owne true fire. Now my thought takes wing,
And now an Epode to deepe eares I sing.

(lines 25–30)

The poet's "true fire" is the fire of intellectual labor, masculine labor as a controlling force, and the phrase "deepe eares" is another reference to the "understanders" whom Jonson graces elsewhere in his work with highest status. This prepares the way for the moral gravitas of "Epode," *Forrest* 11, a poem that celebrates virtuous love and ends with the line "Man may securely sin, but safely, never," a masculine image which Ian Donaldson suggests is a possible reversal of the feminine focus of a line in Seneca,[33] as though to confirm the authority of stoic self-awareness and self-control as masculine. Donaldson has also highlighted the passage at lines 51–54 with its phrase "Preserves community," as an indicator of Jonson's unwavering rational ecumenicism, pointing out that the poem was originally written in Jonson's "Catholic years," but that it was "equally bold of Jonson to have reprinted this poem with its central proposition unchanged in 1616, some years after converting back to the Anglican faith. . . ."[34]

The vehicle of this poetic evocation of virtuous love and ecumenical community is the idea of harnessing reason as a control of the passions, an idea that has classical antecedents but that gained momentum in the seventeenth century through the notion of "interest" as a passion to control the other passions, as Albert O. Hirschman has explained.[35] Donaldson points to Thomas Wright's *The Passions of the Mind in General* (1601) as a possible source. I would suggest, in addition, that we have here one of many indications of Jonson's affinity with Bacon. It is "wakeful reason, our affections king," a version of reason that does not repress the data of sense perception but controls such data: "'Tis the securest policy we have / To make our sense our slave. / But this true course

---

[33] Ian Donaldson, ed. *Ben Jonson: Poems* (Oxford: Oxford Univ. Press, 1975), 107n.

[34] Donaldson, *Ben Jonson: A Life*, 256.

[35] Albert O. Hirschman, *The Passions and the Interests: Political Arguments for Capitalism Before its Triumph* (Princeton, NJ: Princeton Univ. Press, 1978).

is not embraced by many / By many? Scarce by any." The word "sense" is repeated twice in the poem, first as sensation here, and later (line 115) "sense" as reason, or perhaps as rational self-interest in Hirschman's interpretation. Here again there is a suggestion of Bacon's "idols" as, in Bacon's several metaphors, clouds or cobwebs or a distorting mirror of the mind that inhibit the proper role of reason. And ultimately, in this poem the source of right reason and virtuous love is one that Bacon also envisioned: Nature, in the figure of "a person like our dove / Graced with a phoenix's love" . . . "A body so harmoniously composed / As if nature disclosed / All her best symmetry in that one feature!" This is a figure some would read as associated with the Holy Spirit; if so, then the Holy Spirit is gendered here as feminine. But it is doubtful that Jonson would have been so unparochial, and it would hardly be consistent for Jonson to be doing here what Aemilia Lanyer did, in Amy Greenstadt's perceptive reading of Lanyer's "Description of Cooke-ham," by employing "the language of religious devotion" in a way that "challenges stable gender categories."[36] Rather, this is an instance in which Jonson, like Bacon, is alluding to the contemporary debate over the idea of the decay of nature, and taking the position, as did Bacon, that the sin of Adam and Eve did not corrupt all of nature, but rather that nature understood as reason and virtue combined, is the means of paradise regained, an argument that contributed to the epistemology of the "new philosophy," or new science.[37] Nature as a feminine ideal also appears in Jonson's masque *Mercury Vindicated from the Alchemists at Court,* which was included with *The Forrest* in the 1616 folio and which has a similar theme where Nature is described as "young and fresh," and where she instructs Prometheus "to show [the masquers] they are the creatures of the sun, / That each to other / Is a brother, / And Nature here no stepdame, but a mother." The image fits with other idealized representations of

---

[36] Amy Greenstadt, "Aemilia Lanyer's Pathetic Phallacy," *Journal for Early Modern Cultural Studies,* 8, no. 1 (Spring–Summer 2008): 67–97, 74.

[37] For the debate over the idea of the decay of nature see Victor Harris, *All Coherence Gone* (Chicago: Univ. of Chicago Press, 1949), and Richard Foster Jones, *Ancients and Moderns: A Study of the Rise of the Scientific Movement in Seventeenth Century England,* 2nd ed. (Berkeley: Univ. of California Press, 1961).

motherhood from a masculine, heteronormative perspective in *The
Forrest*. This perspective is reinforced in the last lines of *Epode* (*Forrest* 11):

> What savage, brute affection
> Would not be fearful to offend a dame
> Of this excelling fame?
> Much more a noble and right generous mind,
> To virtuous moods inclined,
> That knows the weight of guilt: he will refrain
> From thoughts of such a strain,
> And to his sense object this sentence ever:
> Man may securely sin, but safely, never.
> (lines 108–16)

The passage concludes by redeeming nature and making it worthy of study (as in Bacon's project of a "great instauration"), but also by reinstating masculine authority over "sense" (reason) and judgment.[38]

In the poem that opens this middle section, *Forrest* 4, "To the World: A Farewell for a Gentle-woman, Vertuous and Noble," the affective tone conveys admiration and strong sympathy on the poet's part. R. E. Pritchard has suggested that the "noble" lady in whose voice this poem was written was Mary Wroth. If true, this would further support my reading of the collection as a whole, as an intricate and conflicted engagement with connotations of the name "Sidney." It might even, perhaps, be evidence of some unease on Jonson's part with the conventional misogyny he nonetheless exploits rhetorically in *The Forrest*. But Pritchard's textual evidence, comparing these lines with passages from Wroth's poems, is too limited to

---

[38] The issue of the feminization of nature and the contradictions in how "mother nature" is represented in Bacon and other figures in early seventeenth-century scientific thought have been discussed extensively. See, e.g., Carolyn Merchant, "The Violence of Impediments: Francis Bacon and the Origin of Experimentation," *Isis: A Journal of the History of Science* 99 (Dec. 2008): 731–60, esp. 739–40; and, for a summary treatment, Peter J. Bowler and Iwan Rhys Morus, *Making Modern Science: A Historical Survey* (Chicago: Univ. of Chicago Press, 2010), esp. 489ff.

substantiate his intriguing claim.[39] The speaker is a woman of the court who expresses through the conventional stage metaphor the familiar Renaissance theme of *contemptus mundi*:

> False world, good-night: since thou hast
>   brought That houre upon my morne of age,
> Hence-forth I quit thee from my thought,
>   My part is ended on thy stage.
>
>   (lines 1–4)

The conclusion provides an antithetical metaphor:

> Nor for my peace will I goe farre,
>   As wandrers doe, that still doe roam,
> But make my strengths, such as they are,
>   Here, in my bosome, and at home.
>
>   (lines 65–68)

Here the domestic image, associated with unfallen nature in opposition to the "studied arts" (line 9) of the opening, reiterates the theme of "dwelling" in *Forrest* 2 and 3. Again, "dwelling" (or "at home") is the metaphor for integrity of being that is, in turn, the basis of the virtue and nobility attributed to the gentlewoman in the poem's title. The emotional force, yet subtlety, of Jonson's language makes this one of the more moving and yet disturbing poems in the collection. As former US Poet Laureate Robert Pinsky has remarked, "Jonson's poem is so plain, so direct and explicit, that a reader might miss its overtones of mystery and mortality." Pinsky suggests that the emotive overtones are an effect of Jonson's identification with the condition of his speaker: "[The Gentlewoman's] privileged worldly position allows her to speak this wonderful and stoical goodbye. (A goodbye that the contentious Jonson—he killed a man in a duel and wrote many an angry epigram—assigns to this woman rather than pretending to claim it for himself)."[40]

---

[39] R. E. Pritchard, "'I Exscribe Your Sonnets': Jonson and Lady Mary Wroth," *Notes and Queries* 44, no. 4 (Dec. 1997): 526–28.

[40] Robert Pinsky, "Lost in Court: How One of Ben Jonson's Masterpieces Found the World by Leaving it Behind," *SLATE*, Aug. 30, 2011, http://www.slate.com/articles/arts/poem/2011/08/lost_in_court.html.

I'm inclined to agree that the affective strength of this poem comes from Jonson's admiration for and identification with his subject. But once again, the price of identification with a patron of rank is paid in another poetic figure of misogyny. Here, even when the conditions defining true nobility are spoken in a female voice, conventions of seventeenth-century discourse override the idealization. The "false" and fallen world addressed by the speaker is also female: "I know too, though thou strut, and paint, / Yet art thou both shrunke up, and old" (lines 13–14). While the reference to cosmetics develops the antithesis between art and nature begun at line 9, it is significant that the stoic gentlewoman's disdain of the world is figured in the conventional masculine contempt for an aging female body.

The implied aggression is amplified and yet softened by the Catullan lyricism in the seductive strains of the two songs to "Celia" that follow (*Forrest* 5 and 6), transposed here from their original context, Volpone's attempted rape of Celia, and reaches a climax in the hardly veiled misogyny of the song "That Women Are but Men's Shaddowes" (*Forrest* 7). Of course, here, as elsewhere in Jonson, the intention may be to employ the satiric element as a foil for the ideal. But on the principle, that satire tends to be contagious, a characteristic identified by Robert C. Elliott in his definitive work on satire and particularly prominent where the target is feminized, I would argue that the satiric treatment of women in *The Forrest*, culminating in the overt misogyny of *Forrest* 7, contaminates the representation of a feminine ideal.[41]

Moreover, the poems of this middle section that present images of women as objects of seduction or satire provide contrast not only for the anonymous gentlewoman of *Forrest* 4 but also for the ladies named in the surrounding poems of praise: Lady Sidney of Penshurst, Lady Wroth, the countess of Rutland, and Lady Aubigny. In reading *The Forrest*, one is struck by the extent to which Jonson's praise of his patrons is focused on their wives and daughters. Barbara (Gamage) Sidney is praised for her "high huswifery," chastity, and maternal devotion; Lady Aubigny is idealized similarly while also depicted as possessing lasting beauty not only of body but of mind, though only after having both subordinated to her husband:

---

[41] Robert C. Elliott, *The Power of Satire: Magic, Ritual, Art* (Princeton, NJ: Princeton Univ. Press, 1960), passim, but see esp. 40–41.

"how still / You are depending on his word and will" (*Forrest* 13, lines 113–14). If, as I contend, the satire of women in *Forrest* 7 is sufficiently generalized to undercut the intended contrast with women praised elsewhere, then we have further evidence of the irony that characterizes the text as a whole. In the overall context of *The Forrest,* the witty misogyny of the song "That Women Are but Men's Shaddowes" constitutes a displacement of another kind of aggression, providing a release of the animus that issues from Jonson's sense of inequity concerning his own social position with respect to the male members of a ruling class whom his poems must serve. The debasement of the courtly ideal of womanhood, and the repudiation of a neo-Platonic poetic tradition associated with that ideal (immediately in *Forrest* 1, "Why I Write Not of Love"), are disguised or deformed gestures of opposition to the class of aristocrats on whom the professional poet must depend.

One qualification of what I have said here: I want to acknowledge Anne Baynes Coiro's point, in referring to Mary Wroth's poetry and to poetry addressed to her by Jonson, that a feminist reading "must take into account not only concepts now shaping our sense of early-modern women such as 'dismemberment' or 'voyeurism' or 'silencing' but also the real power of this and other individual women as part of a social network. In Jonson's representation of Wroth, she rises above the name of wife, her birth heritage so luminous in her writing that she reclaims her Sidney name."[42] Also, by placing Jonson's position in relation to his female patrons alongside Aemilia Lanyer's similar relation (on the basis of class if not of gender), Coiro shrewdly sees a certain commonality between them. Of Lanyer, she writes: "A crucial part of her social radicalism is that Lanyer is writing as a *woman* writer to aristocratic women; her writing is as edgy, self-fashioning, and socially self-conscious as Jonson's ever is. We cannot read her right unless we read her sophisticated irony about her position in a world where she is dependent on a matriarchy she often resents. . . . Both Lanyer and Jonson lived dependent on these women and, to a large extent, their writing personalities were generated by the resentments and needs that

---

[42] Ann Baynes Coiro, "Writing in Service: Sexual Politics and Class Position in the Poetry of Aemilia Lanyer and Ben Jonson," *Criticism,* 35, no. 3 (Summer 1993): 357–76.

these service relationships created. . . . Placing Jonson's anger next to Lanyer's . . . should destabilize any simple sense of gender wars" (365–66). Coiro's point is related to the broader subject analyzed by Jean Howard in addressing the question that forms the title of her essay, "Was There a Renaissance Feminism?," to which Howard provides a complex and persuasive reply dealing with both the gender and class issues involved in the question.[43] This may be a mitigating factor in Jonson's favor, but unlike, Lanyer, Jonson's poetic persona and his politics are not "radical." His politics, though contestatory, are reformist, and to that end he was either unwilling to suppress a compromise of his meritocratic ethic on the issue of gender, or ignorant of the fact that he did so compromise.

The Doctrine of Things Indifferent

I began this essay with an epigraph from Horace's *Ars Poetica*, a passage Sidney also highlighted in his *Defence*, though he offered no English translation. I was intrigued by the fact that of all the subsequent English translations, Jonson's, which may be the first, is the only one that renders "*mediocribus*" as "indifferent." Most translations use "mediocrity" or "mediocre," which is understandable given the context, a passage in which a greater latitude for error is said to be tolerated in such professions as law or politics than in poetry. But Jonson also alters the connotation of Horace's original to suggest that with poets a tolerance of occasional, small error must not compromise an overall capacity for judgment.[44] Checking *OED* I found that "mediocrity" is indeed given as a like term for "indifferent," but it is only a very subordinate meaning, not a principal one. Jonson's use of "indifferent" in this context gives his line greater force than Horace's, by granting greater authority and responsibility to the poet.

---

[43] Jean E. Howard, "Was There a Renaissance Feminism?," in *A Companion to English Renaissance Literature and Culture*, ed. Michael Hattaway (Oxford: Blackwell, 2000), 644–52.

[44] Victoria Moul analyzes other instances of Jonson's deviations and elaborations from Horace in her impressive book *Jonson, Horace and the Classical Tradition* (Cambridge: Cambridge University Press, 2010).

That Jonson chose the term "indifferent" may have been as an allusion to its use by contemporaries in translating the Stoic, Pyrrhonist, or Christian versions of *adiaphora*. Jonson shifts the burden of meaning from Horace's denial that a poet can be mediocre and still be considered a poet to a denial that a poet can be ethically indifferent. If Jonson is alluding to the "doctrine of things indifferent," which had many competing and contradictory interpretations in seventeenth-century theological and political debates, then it is ostensibly to the way that doctrine was understood by the Anglican church and its highest authority, the king. According to Anglican interpretation the authority to adjudicate among "things indifferent" is derived by the king from God. Jonson sometimes identifies the poet, whom he calls a "maker" from the Greek *poiein* (to make), with that authority, as did Sidney when he wrote in the *Defence* of "the heavenly Maker of that maker." If the king is the final judge among "things indifferent," then hidden perhaps in the subtle shift in meaning of the above passage translating Horace is a not so subtle allusion to and appropriation of that power of judgment for the poet.[45] The poet, then, like the king, is not "indifferent," because his is the ultimate authority to adjudicate a difference among "things indifferent." I believe, too, that it is not inconsistent with seventeenth-century usage to say that as Jonson employs it, "indifferent" can imply "disinterested" or even "disengaged."

Jonson's poet is interested and engaged like Milton after him, though with different motive and agenda. Jonson's reference to "the doctrine of things indifferent" is hardly embedded in religious controversy to the degree that Milton's references would be a generation later, and Jonson's rhetorical allusion is not so elaborate as Milton's later rhetorical turns on the doctrine as analyzed by Stanley Fish and Victoria Kahn.[46] Milton's rhetoric is complex and even seems

---

[45] On Jonson's identification of the poet's "authorial capacity for aesthetic and moral judgment with the king's juridical power in relation to his subjects," see Don E. Wayne, "Drama and Society in the Age of Jonson: An Alternative View," *Renaissance Drama* N.S. 13 (1982): 103–29 (esp. 117–18).

[46] Fish, "Things and Actions Indifferent: The Temptation of Plot in *Paradise Regained*," *Milton Studies* 17 (1983), 163–85; Stanley Fish, "Driving from the Letter: Truth and Indeterminacy in Milton's *Areopagitica*," in

to employ strategic self-contradiction in places, as Kahn has shown in her incisive reading of *Aereopagitica*. She writes:

> ... both supporters and critics of the status quo equated the realm of things indifferent with the jurisdiction of established authorities. Thus, supporters tried to enlarge the area of indifference while dissenters restricted it, often claiming that nothing was indifferent to the individual believer. Milton's intervention in this debate is far more rhetorically sophisticated than the usual positions in that he uses the argument of his presbyterian opponents against themselves: he enlarges the realm of indifference to criticize rather than support Episcopacy and he does so by making indifference a matter of individual judgment.[47]

Kahn goes on to suggest that "For Milton in this text knowledge is dialectical: it proceeds by contraries. And in this dialectical process is itself described as 'incessant labor' or ... a 'race' or 'trial.'" Illustrative of this process is Milton's own "anxiety ... [and] ambivalent rhetoric when discussing human agency. In the dialectic of the argument, as soon as Milton stresses individual agency and the exercise of individual judgment, he draws back to assert the existence and efficaciousness of objective truth" (552–53).

Re-membering Milton, ed. Mary Nyquist and Margaret W. Ferguson (New York: Methuen, 1988); Victoria Kahn, "Allegory, the Sublime, and the Rhetoric of Things Indifferent in *Paradise Lost*" in *Creative Imitation: New Essays on Renaissance Literature in Honor of Thomas M. Greene*, ed. David Quint et al. (Binghamton: MRTS, 1992), 127–52; and Kahn, "Revising the History of Machiavellism: English Machiavellism and the Doctrine of Things Indifferent," *RQ* 46, no. 3 (1993): 526–61, especially her discussion of Milton's engagement with the doctrine in *Aereopagitica*. I am grateful to Ward Risvold, a Latinist and lexicographer and a judicious scholar of early modern print culture, for his advice and support of this reading of Jonson's use of "indifferent," and to Mike Burch for helpful bibliography and conversation related to this question.

[47] Kahn, "Revising the History of Machiavellism," 550.

Epistemology and Experiment

Despite differences in motive, I believe something similar can be said of Jonson's rhetoric with regard to the relation between human agency and the criterion of objective truth, and in his association of truth with a process involving "incessant labor," a "race" or "trial." Milton's consistent motive is theological as well as political and philosophical. Jonson is also political and philosophical, but, I would argue, he is motivated less by theology and more by pragmatic epistemological and ethical concerns. His concept of the poet as an ultimate arbiter of "things indifferent" is related to the Baconian ideas he invokes in his Preface to the *English Grammar* (ca. 1623): his poems (and his plays which he thought of as "poems") are experiments embodying the principles, "Experience, Observation, Sense, Induction" he calls the "Tryers of Arts."[48] Jonson's epistemology, like Bacon's and Hobbes's, is protoscientific. He conceives of the poet as an explorer, an experimenter, a discoverer, an innovator, on the model of Bacon's concept of the "new" philosopher or scientist. At the same time, given the absolutist political context in which Jonson sought validation of his intellect and identity, he could not anticipate later scientific claims to a value neutral epistemology. Epistemology and ethics are, as in Bacon, complementary aspects of "new philosophy" as they are of Jonson's "strange" new poetry, and they are part of a grand program for education and social improvement, though one with more socially marked ranks and exclusions on Bacon's part, in keeping with his aristocratic position. Jonson too enlarges the realm of indifference that ostensibly supports the jurisdiction of king and court, but he also subverts that authority by shifting the seat of judgment to those qualified by the most honorable title of intellectual merit.

I view Jonson as an experimental writer, and I argue, contrary to those who view him as profoundly traditional and conservative, that in this respect he was not only "early modern" but "postmodern." Everything I've written previously about Ben Jonson has been driven by the idea that he was developing what was a fundamentally experimental aesthetic, one that was as modern as it was reliant on ancient forms, one that even has elements of the postmodern in

---

[48] Ben Jonson, *English Grammar*, H & S, VIII, 465.

the sense understood by Jean-Francois Lyotard, with the example of Montaigne's essays, that is, in the sense of a constant *trying*:

> Postmodernism thus understood is not modernism at its end but in the nascent state, and this state is constant.... A postmodern artist or writer is in the position of a philosopher: the text he writes, the work he produces are not in principle governed by preestablished rules, and they cannot be judged according to a determining judgment, by applying familiar categories to the text or to the work. Those rules and categories are what the work of art itself is looking for. The artist and the writer, then, are working without rules in order to formulate the rules of what *will have been done*.[49]

The idea of Jonson as in this sense "postmodern" may seem absurd, but it is an element in one of the best essays I have read on Jonson's poetry, by a non-Jonson specialist, a poet herself whose sensitivity to nuances of language and to the element of the sublime in Jonson is something exceptional, Linda Gregerson.[50] She begins her study with a striking and surprising move, likening Jonson's attitude to language, to interpretation, and to the reader, to the attitude of Samuel Beckett. Gregerson's reading of the final poem in *The Forrest*, "To Heaven" (*For.*, 15), one of the rare devotional poems in the Jonson canon, is especially compelling by its unorthodoxy. If there is a theological dimension to Jonson's writing, I believe it is one expressed equivocally. Of all the critical commentary I have read on the few devotional poems he wrote, including "To Heaven," the most perceptive, and the most moving to me is Gregerson's, because it most successfully evokes Jonson's struggle with religion by recognizing and sharing his struggle with language, and by likening that fundamentally epistemological struggle to Beckett's.

Yet, by the standard of "what will have been done" Jonson's claim that the poet cannot be "indifferent" is compromised by the

---

[49] Jean-Francois Lyotard, "Answering the Question: What Is Postmodernism?," trans. Regis Durand, *The Postmodern Condition: A Report on Knowledge* (Minneapolis: Univ. of Minnesota Press, 1984), 71–82.

[50] Linda Gregerson, "Ben Jonson and the Loathéd Word," in *Green Thoughts, Green Shades: Essays by Contemporary Poets on the Early Modern Lyric*, ed. Jonathan F. S. Post (Berkeley: Univ. of California Press, 2002), 86–108.

inconsistency of his meritocratic ethic which remains hierarchical, exclusionary, and conventionally and conveniently framed in terms of gender. There is a part of me, however, that would like to imagine Jonson employing self-contradiction in a manner like Milton, playing the strains of misogyny throughout *The Forrest* as a deliberate rhetorical strategy to challenge readers to discern for themselves the ethical inconsistency. That would make his book a remarkably dialectical achievement ahead of its time. It would also make Jonson a true exemplar of the "postmodern," which, says Lyotard, "would have to be understood according to the paradox of the future *(post)* anterior *(modo)*."[51] But, *pace* Lyotard, that would also be to indulge in some romantic wishfulness, wistfulness, and anachronism of my own making.

Anachronism and Alibi: Time's Up!

Readers who may be put off by what I have said about the thread of misogyny in Jonson's *The Forrest*, and who may think that I am indeed being anachronistic in raising this issue or in reading it as symptomatic of sublimated class antagonism in the system of patronage, might ask themselves whether to deny manifestations of seventeenth-century forms of such behaviors is to replicate misogyny in the present and to contribute to the justification of what we now call by the neutralizing euphemism "income inequality" in the twenty-first century. Anachronism is a potential danger in any moralistic criticism. In some cases, however, when the charge of "anachronism" is levelled at a retrospective use of current categories of analysis, as in the case of some objections years ago when Raymond Williams used cultural studies categories based on Marx's social theory to analyze seventeenth-century estate poems, the objection is part of an ideology of forgetting, and therefore, itself, unhistorical.[52] It might be a distortion of Jonson's writing in *The Forrest* to make an unqualified affirmative claim about his focus on women in this collection, but it is certainly not anachronistic to employ the

---

[51] Lyotard, "Answering the Question," 81.

[52] I refer to some critics' comments on Williams's *The Country and the City* (New York: Oxford Univ. Press, 1973).

term "misogyny" with respect to these poems. It is not anachronistic to question the judgment of critics who would exclude the epithets "misogyny" or "exploitation of labor" from Renaissance and early modern literary criticism and historiography, on the grounds that such terms were not current in the discourse of the period. Those who charge that this is a form of anachronism are themselves participating in a kind of forgetfulness that represses retrospective empirical historical evidence for the sake of preserving untarnished a nostalgic ideal.

Another vantage point from which to reply to the charge of anachronism is presented by Edward Said, though in relation to a different context, the postcolonial writer's antithetical relation to what is still a vital element in the colonial literary tradition. Replying to critics who would dismiss Joseph Conrad's Eurocentric depictions of nineteenth-century colonialism and racism, Said writes, with reference to *Heart of Darkness*:

> ... I am always trying to understand figures from the past whom I admire, even as I point out how bound they were by the perspectives of their own cultural moment as far as their views of other cultures and peoples were concerned.... My approach tries to see them in their context as accurately as possible, but then—because they are extraordinary writers and thinkers whose work has enabled other, alternative work and readings based on developments of which they could not have been aware—I see them contrapuntally, that is, as figures whose writing travels across temporal, cultural, and ideological boundaries in unforeseen ways to emerge as part of a new ensemble along with later history and subsequent art.... Thus later history reopens and challenges what seems to have been the finality of an earlier figure of thought, bringing it into contact with cultural, political and epistemological formations undreamed of by—albeit affiliated by historical circumstances with—its author.... Texts that are inertly of their time stay there: those which brush up unstintingly against historical constraints are the ones we keep with us, generation after generation.[53]

---

[53] Edward Said, *The Selected Works of Edward Said, 1966–2006*, ed. Moustafa Bayoumi and Andrew Rubin (New York: Vintage Books, 2019), 502.

Jonson's texts (contrary to some opinion in the dominant critical tradition) are NOT "inertly of their time," but are rather the kinds of texts that "brush up unstintingly against historical constraints," even if they never quite break those constraints.

The factors that generate misogyny, racism, homophobia, child abuse, and other forms of repression are too complex to be reduced to an effect of class conflict, as I'm suggesting was at least one motive of Jonson's misogyny. But in times when culture and ideology are in the process of being decoded and destabilized, as they were in the seventeenth century around religious and political issues, and as they are in similar yet historically different ways today, ancient and traditional repressive structures become weapons in battles over other kinds of issues governing social relations. Exemplary are the seventeenth-century conflicts in England that climaxed in armed struggle over material social conditions and their ideological expressions in politics, religion, law, and literature; that is, conflict among what Williams termed "dominant, residual and emergent structures of feeling"[54] surrounding the question of where sovereignty is to be located, and who is to be included and who excluded in the "emergent" response to that question.

I do not mean to suggest that Jonson's misogyny can be explained solely on the grounds of a displaced class antagonism, but rather that there is an interrelationship between these animating factors in his writing and that together they constitute a significant determinant of the condescending attitude to women that pervades this book. Indeed, the women who are named and praised in *The Forrest* are treated as the shadows of the fathers and husbands to whom they belong. They exemplify an ideal of womanhood in which passion and power are contained. If the misogyny of *Forrest* 7 is a displacement of Jonson's own alienation and of his hostility to the class he serves, then the poems in praise of female members of that class express an identification with the ruling patriarchy from which the poet is excluded on the basis of rank but not on the basis of gender. While genealogy is necessarily alluded to in these poems, a primary vehicle of praise is the depiction of the patron's wife as a model of domestic and conjugal duty. The representation

---

[54] Raymond Williams, *Marxism and Literature* (Oxford: Oxford Univ. Press, 1977), 127.

of dutiful wives is an essential part of the ideology that *The Forrest*
helps produce, an ideology of patriarchal domesticity that includes
the emergent notion of the nuclear family as the origin and foundation of order in society. Jonson's images of domesticity, though here
immediately associated with the estates of his patrons (Penshurst,
Durrance), have wider application: they depend on the concept of a
"universal nature" that cuts across class distinctions. Superimposed
upon the patron's house (in both the architectural and the gene-
alogical senses of the term) is the category of the home, a "natural" community in which gender rather than genealogy determines
rank. But the form in which this ideology is shaped in Ben Jonson's
The Forrest is a "broken backed" form, a form in which the analytic
propositional statement of such a concept of "universal nature" is
contradicted by the dialectical logic in the structural irony of this
sequence of fifteen poems.

The broken-backed form discloses the ideological nature of
what is represented elsewhere in *The Forrest* as "universal nature."
It functions as what Marin attributes to utopian discourse, as mod-
eled in Thomas More's *Utopia*: that is, as an "ideological critique of
ideology." Even a work that reproduces a repressive ideology may
be so structured as to enable an epistemological reflexivity that
seeks to expand the relevant contexts of what is meant by epistemology. In our own time we are in dire need of such reflexivity as
a means toward engaging creatively and constructively in improv-
ing the dangerous conditions that confront the world's natural,
social, cultural ecosystems.[55] In this respect, a watchword that has
gained currency in the most recent feminist critique of the persistent destructive effects of patriarchy, is worth expanding to other
relevant contexts—"Time's up!"

University of California, San Diego

---

[55] For a theoretical and practical approach to this epistemological
and ethical issue, see the discussion of "reflexivity in normativity" as this
concept relates to disciplinary and professional institutions in Aleksan-
dar Jokic, *International Justice After the Cold War: Essays with Applications*,
American University Studies, Series V: Philosophy, v. 230 (New York:
Peter Lang, 2018), xvi–xvii, 10–15, and passim.